W9-CHO-976

What Others Are Saying About River Dwellers

On rare occasions a book touches me so deeply that I need time to articulate what I experienced or encountered while reading it. *River Dwellers* is one of those books. There are no words to express how much I appreciate what Dr. Rob Reimer has written — *River Dwellers* is a text that awakens a hunger for the manifest presence of God. The spiritual passion with which he writes is imparted to the reader through the page. May God use it for His glory. Amen.

Rev. Tom Ward
Director of Ministry Operations
Vision Nationals
Ridgway, CO

The Lord has used Dr. Rob Reimer, his ministry, and his books to draw me into a deeper and deeper intimacy with Himself. River Dwellers is an excellent resource for developing the ability to hear God's quiet whispers and live in a moment-by-moment dynamic relationship with the Lord Jesus Christ.

Rev. Jeff Norris
District Superintendent
Western Pennsylvania District in the Christian and Missionary Alliance
Punxsutawney, PA

The term "River Dweller" strikes a chord with my soul. If you are like me, after reading this book, you will want to get in the River and stay there! All my adult life, I have stressed that Christ followers must "walk in the Spirit," but that phrase left my soul longing for a better way of saying, "God takes pleasure in us when we rest in Him." We must decide to remain in Him, but living in the River is less about human efforts of striding and striving and more about being and resting, thus letting God's Spirit wash over, under, and all around us.

This book is about a quest that satisfies... the quest of remaining in the River where you will find an infinite God, and thus, there is always more of Him to experience. Take the plunge, and you will never again be satisfied living on the bank.

Rev. Tom Mangham
Director of Spiritual Life Development & Advanced Theological Studies
Evangelism Explosion International
Arden, North Carolina

My friend Rob Reimer is a "River Dweller." He loves to soak in God's presence and experience God's power. Rob is not one of those guys who writes about the River from the safety of the dry bank. He is not content with writing about other people's experiences in the River. No, Rob is a man who is hungry for God and will jump into the River every chance he gets. By the way, he likes to cannonball into the River so he can get as many people wet as possible! That's one of the reasons I love him. My life is wet with the presence of Jesus in large measure because of my relationship with Rob Reimer.

Dr. Ron Walborn
Dean of Alliance Theological Seminary
Nyack, NY

River Dwellers

Living in the Fullness of the Spirit

Dr. Rob Reimer

Carpenter's Son Publishing

River Dwellers: Living in the Fullness of the Spirit

© 2015 by Rob Reimer

No part of this book may be reproduced or transmitted in any form or by any means, electronic or mechanical, including photocopying, recording or by any information storage and retrieval system, without permission in writing from the copyright owner.

All scripture taken from the The Holy Bible, Today's New International Version® unless otherwise noted. Copyright © 2001, 2005 by Biblica®. Used by permission of Biblica®. All rights reserved worldwide.

Published by Carpenter's Son Publishing, Franklin, Tennessee

Published in association with Larry Carpenter of Christian Book Services, LLC
www.christianbookservices.com

Edited by Tammy Kling

Cover Design by John Pepe

Interior Layout Design by Mark Neubauer

Printed in the United States of America

978-1-940262-78-9

All rights reserved.

Acknowledgements

Years ago I was sitting in my doctoral class, and Dr. Haddon Robinson made a comment. He said, "Gentlemen, there are only about 15 major themes in Scripture." Of course, everyone in the class wanted to know what the 15 themes were. But that wasn't the question that consumed me. The question that burned in my mind was, "How do you stay in one place for a long time if you preach to a group of people on only 15 themes?" I heard the Spirit of God whisper to me, "You must go deep. There is infinite depth in those 15 themes." I took it to heart.

I went to the board of South Shore Community Church and told them this story. I asked them to consider giving me a study break each summer if they wanted me to stay for the long haul so I could have focused time to pursue God, study, and go deep. I'm in my 20th year at SSCC, and I am indebted to those people of faith that I have served alongside for all these years. That study break has been a great aid to my attempts to live in the River. Thank you for all your support over the years, board members, staff, and South Shore friends!

A special thanks to Fred and Karen White and Dave and Barb MacBeth. Thank you for believing in me and supporting me to make this book possible. I couldn't have done it without you.

Andi Long, you are a gift from God to me! You have managed two book projects now, and you have been a superb help from start to finish both times. You have been an editor, friend, cheerleader, project manager and have done it all with an unrelentingly gracious attitude. Thank you can't even begin to cover the gratitude I feel for you!

Jen, I am usually in front of a crowd by virtue of my calling, but you are the glue behind the scenes that holds everything together. For nearly 25 years, you have been my most worthy partner and made our home a refuge. When I think of you, I think of Charles Dickens' great description of Mrs. Fezziwig, "As to her, she was worthy to be his partner in every sense of the term. If that's not high praise, tell me higher, and I'll use it." You are a noble lady, and I am a lucky man!

Danielle, Courtney, Darcy and Craig — I am proud of you guys! I'm glad God gave you to me. You are all growing up, and it has been a joy to be your Dad.

Dedication

I dedicate this book to my friend, Dr. Martin Sanders. In 1991, I sat in the back row of my last class in Alliance Theological Seminary as I finished up my MDiv, and you were the young visiting professor. I instantly connected with you, as so many people do. Who would have guessed what would have become of that providential encounter? For nearly twenty years, we have partnered together, taught together, and ministered together. We have watched God do miracles, witnessed the captives get set free, and watched lives be transformed by the power of Jesus. We have laughed together, cried together, prayed together, and walked through life together. We have shared our hearts and souls. I consider our friendship to be one of the great honors and privileges of my life. In this last season, as you cared for Dianna in her final years through her illness, I watched you serve her in ways that inspired me, and I saw God shape you in ways that moved me to tears. I've never been prouder to call you my friend. You have been a River Dweller, and the presence of God in your life has created spiritual thirst in countless numbers of people who have come into close proximity with you — including me. Thank you, friend.

Table of Contents

"Where the river flows everything will live."

Ezekiel 47:9

Introduction

I grew up in a conservative evangelical church. The people were good people, and I am grateful for their influence in my life. But what I experienced in that little Christian and Missionary Alliance Church in Poughkeepsie, New York didn't resemble the book of Acts very much.

I only remember one person coming to faith in Christ — and that was my dad when I was about 11. I don't remember any dramatic, life-change testimonies. I can't recall anyone being miraculously healed. I don't ever remember anyone telling stories of great life-altering encounters with God. The people in that church were good people, but they weren't making much of an impact in their community.

Jesus wasn't making much of an impact in my life at that time, either. I went to church and had friends there, but it didn't affect the way I lived. Not that I gave Him much of a chance — He took a back seat to most of my activities and was rather peripheral.

That changed when I was 19 years old. I was dating a girl from church, and we broke up. It was a devastating blow to me at the time. As I drove home that night, I pulled over to the side of the road and cried out to God. And much to my surprise, God met me.

I cried out, "God, I gave this girl my heart, and now look what happened!" As I cried out to God, I sensed the Spirit of God speak to my heart. I heard the Spirit say, "That is the same way you have treated me." I had a picture of Jesus pursuing me, arms open wide, ready to embrace me, and me pushing Him to the side. I felt deep conviction, my tears moved from tears of self-pity to tears of repentance, and I surrendered my life to Christ. I said, "From now on, you lead; I follow. You've got me; I'm yours."

 As I prayed those words through tears of conviction, the Spirit of God filled me. I felt an overwhelming sense of the love of God flooding my soul. I felt a deep joy bubbling up within me. It was the Spirit of God releasing love and joy into my soul like I had never experienced before. That day completely changed my life. I had never heard anyone talk about having an encounter with God like that, and I had certainly never encountered God's manifest presence before in my own life. I didn't know what to call it. I didn't know how to describe it. All I knew was God visited me, and I changed.

After I had this encounter with God, I told a few people from church about it. I was on fire for God for the first time in my life. But the first few people I told did not encourage me. They all said things like this: "Don't put too much stock in the experience." "Feelings come and go." "This too will pass." "Don't be worried when the feelings pass — that's normal." It didn't exactly throw fuel on my fire! It actually discouraged me and made me a little gun shy to talk about my encounter with God.

As I continued processing this experience, I began to ask myself two questions: What was this experience? And how do I stay connected to God like this for the long haul? I figured out the answer to the first question in seminary and through studying the Scriptures, the history of revivals, and some very helpful books. I discovered this experience was the Baptism of the Holy Spirit.

The second question has been the pursuit of a lifetime. How do I experience the ongoing abundant life Jesus promised — the deep, intimate, satisfying connection with the living God? What I've discovered is living in the fullness of the Spirit is the key. Throughout this book, we will explore what it means to be baptized by the Spirit, and we'll discuss how to remain in the fullness of the Spirit.

The Baptism of the Spirit

Being baptized by the Spirit at age 19 changed the course of my life. Before that encounter, I had never considered ministry as a profession, but after that supernatural experience with God, I felt like Jeremiah. Jeremiah says, "His word is in my heart like a fire, a fire shut up in my bones. I am weary of holding it in; indeed, I cannot" (Jeremiah 20:9). I felt called — compelled by the Spirit — and I pursued a career in ministry.

I was 23 when I went to seminary and heard Dr. Terry Wardle talk about "the filling of the Holy Spirit." As he described it, I finally had terminology for what I experienced at 19. It didn't make me satisfied, though. Listening to him teach about the filling of the Spirit made me more hungry for God. I wanted a fresh encounter with God, and I wanted to live in the fullness of the Spirit I had experienced.

I began studying the baptism, or filling, of the Spirit in more depth. I realized the entire success of the church in Acts could be traced back to this baptism of the Spirit. After the Spirit was poured out on the 120 followers of Jesus on the day of Pentecost (Acts 2), the small band of disciples became an unstoppable force for the advancement of the Kingdom of God. The sick were healed. The demonized were set free. The dead were raised, and people came to faith in Christ every day. Christ was formed in those believers, and they were willing to follow Jesus to the ends of the earth. Everywhere they went they left their mark. Without the baptism of the Spirit, they would not have even been remembered.

In order to bear fruit and have a culture-changing impact as a church today, we must be filled with the Spirit like the early disciples. Not only must we be filled with the Spirit, but we must also live in the present fullness of the Spirit. This isn't a pentecostal or charismatic thing. I know evangelicals who are living in the fullness of the Spirit, and I know charismatics who have the theology for it but not the practice of it. All believers, regardless of their theological persuasion, need to live in the current reality of the Spirit's fullness, or the church will continue to decline in numbers and in its influence to shape culture in America.

I recognize the baptism of the Spirit has been a controversial topic much disputed in the church. If the key to the success of the church in Acts was the baptism of the Spirit, I think we need to look at this with an open mind. I think we would be wise to wrestle with this, laying aside our preconceived notions. We should be less concerned with defending our theological positions and more concerned about living in the reality Jesus spoke about in the Gospels — the reality the early church lived out in the book of Acts.

The early disciples were Spirit people, and we need to become Spirit people. We clearly are not enjoying the success of the early church, and we could desperately use their supernatural empowerment. When the early church experienced the baptism of the Spirit, it created a spiritual earthquake that changed the spiritual landscape of the Roman Empire. We are desperate for that kind of impact today.

River Dwellers

The key to remaining in the fullness of the Spirit is dwelling in the River of Life. Jesus said in John 7:37-38, "If anyone is thirsty, let him come to me and drink. Whoever believes in me, as the Scripture has said, streams of living water will flow from within him." In verse 39, John explains that Jesus was referring to the Spirit of God who would come and dwell in us who believe. The promise of Jesus is the Spirit of God would flow within us like a river; He is the River of Life, and we must become River Dwellers. We must dwell full-time in the River of Life where the fullness of God flows. If we are going to experience the abundant life Jesus promised, we must learn how to live in this River.

God doesn't fill us with His Spirit just for our own benefit — He fills us to spill us. He wants to fill us with Living Water so we can spill Living Water wherever we go, just like the early disciples did. He wants to fill us so those dying of spiritual thirst may drink of the Living Water.

All around us there are people who are dying of spiritual thirst. Most do not even know it, but that doesn't change the reality of the spiritual longings which are deep within their hearts. They turn to many things to satisfy these deep longings, but none quench. We cannot be like them and turn to the unsatisfactory wells the world offers. We must be different. We must be Spirit people who learn to drink deeply from the River that satis-fies — not just occasionally; we must make a habit of drinking this Living Water. Then we must offer that life-giving Water to all who surround us.

Ultimately, there is only one number that matters to God. It is the number zero. We live in a broken world full of unsatisfied longings, sin, and pain. When Jesus returns, He will put an end to evil, and all of its side effects, and He will fulfill all the promises of God. Some, even in the apostle Peter's day and age, wondered why Jesus took so long to return. Why doesn't He come and put an end to evil now? Why doesn't He come and satisfy our souls with His presence and love now? 2 Peter 3:9 answers the question of why He delays: "The Lord is not slow in keeping his promise, as some understand slowness. Instead he is patient with you, not wanting anyone to perish, but everyone to come to repentance."

The Lord delays because He doesn't want anyone to be spiritually sepa-rated from His Father. He delays so we can get as close to zero as possible. It is the one number near and dear to the heart of God: ZERO. If the church is going to get close to zero, then the people of God must get in the River! We will not get close to zero because of our innovation, strategy, or vision. Those things are important, and I don't minimize them. But the zero factor of the church is utterly dependent upon the water level of the Spirit in the lives of God's people. If we make our best effort without the filling of the

Spirit, it won't make much difference. Jesus said apart from Him we could do nothing. If we do our best with the fullness of the Spirit together, we can close in on zero for the glory of God.

The disciples in the church of Acts learned to dwell in the River. They were baptized with the Spirit, and they walked in the fullness of the Spirit. Look at the impact they made. They turned the Roman Empire upside down because they were Spirit people, and the water level of the Spirit was high in their lives. We are not making the impact today the early disciples made then because what was true of them is not true of enough of us. We need revival — a fresh outpouring of the Spirit in our midst, and we need to pursue this baptism and fullness of the Spirit.

Revival is a Spirit-filled community of believers. It is a community of believers who have been filled with the Spirit and are continuing to live in the fullness of the Spirit. It is a community of people who have become full-time River Dwellers together.

We desperately need another movement of the Spirit in our lifetime. If we are going to see revival, we need a Spirit-filled community — an ever increasing number of people walking in the present fullness of God. We need an army of Spirit-filled people advancing God's Kingdom.

I pray this book will increase your desire to be a River-Dwelling, Spirit-filled person in the Kingdom of God and will give you practical help for the journey. May it create a passionate thirst for God within your soul which launches you on a quest for the River of Life.

"I was all the time tugging and carrying water, but now I have a river that carries me."

D.L. Moody

"You will receive power when the Holy Spirit comes on you; and you will be my witnesses in Jerusalem, and in all Judea and Samaria, and to the ends of the earth."

Acts 1: 8

CHAPTER 1

The River Gushes:

The Baptism of the Holy Spirit

Jesus taught us about the "baptism of the Holy Spirit." He told His disciples in Acts 1:4-5, 8 to "Wait for the gift my Father promised, which
you have heard me speak about. For John baptized with water, but in a few
days you will be baptized with the Holy Spirit... You will receive power
when the Holy Spirit comes on you; and you will be my witnesses in Jerusalem, and in all Judea and Samaria, and to the ends of the earth."

It's important to distinguish between *receiving* the Holy Spirit and being
baptized by the Spirit. Martyn Lloyd-Jones argues in *Joy Unspeakable* that
these disciples who were awaiting the baptism of the Spirit had already
received the Holy Spirit. The Spirit was already indwelling them, as we see
in John 20:21-22: "Jesus said, 'Peace be with you! As the Father has sent me,
I am sending you.' And with that he breathed on them and said, 'Receive
the Holy Spirit.'"

When we repent of our sin and put our faith in Christ alone for forgiveness and salvation, we become a Christian, and the Holy Spirit takes
up residence in our spirit — we receive the Holy Spirit. That's what makes
us a Christian: the Spirit of God indwells us and brings us new life. This
is regeneration; it is also referred to as the new birth. Every believer has
received the Holy Spirit.

In the famous conversation Jesus had with Nicodemus in John chapter

3, Jesus talks about the new birth. He told Nicodemus we could not enter the Kingdom of God unless we were born again. Nicodemus took it literally and was confused. Jesus explains:

"'Very truly I tell you, no one can enter the kingdom of God without being born of water and the Spirit. Flesh gives birth to flesh, but the Spirit gives birth to spirit. You should not be surprised at my saying, 'You must be born again.' The wind blows wherever it pleases. You hear its sound, but you cannot tell where it comes from or where it is going. So it is with everyone born of the Spirit'" (John 3:7, 8).

Just as we were born into our human families with the breaking of our mother's water and the birth process, so we must be born spiritually into God's family. Our natural birth comes through our earthly mother, but our spiritual birth comes through our Heavenly Father. The spiritual birth occurs when we repent of our sin and turn to Christ for salvation and forgiveness. We lean totally on Him in active faith for a relationship with the Father and an eternal home in Heaven. We don't trust in our goodness, or in our efforts, or in our church affiliation to reconcile us to the Father. We trust in the merits of Jesus' death and resurrection alone for the forgiveness of our sins.

The Spirit of God does an internal change in our lives when we put our faith in Christ. He gives us a new heart, a new Spirit — He puts His Spirit in us, and we become children of God. We are born spiritually into the family of God.

Jesus says the work of the Spirit is like the wind. You can't see the wind, but you can see its effects. I am sitting outside as I write. It is a beautiful day, and the wind is blowing gently. I can't actually see the wind, but I can see the effects of the wind as it moves the branches on the trees. I can hear it blowing through the leaves. This is how it is with the new life in Christ which begins with the indwelling of the Spirit. The change takes place in our hearts and renders change in our lives. God begins a work inside of us that works its way outside of us.

As we mature in our faith, we begin to see the effects of the Spirit in our life. He renders an inner change that leads to an outward transformation. We experience conviction when we sin and offend God with our attitudes and behaviors, and we desire to walk with God and to know God. He gives us a new heart, and it results in new attitudes and patterns of behavior.

Through the work of the Spirit, over time, we become less selfish and more service oriented; we become less greedy and more generous. We become less angry and more forgiving; we become less demanding and more compassionate. This is all the work of the Spirit blowing in our lives. No one can see when we are born spiritually into the family of God but, if the wind of God is blowing in our lives, people should be able to see the effects of the Spirit's activity within us.

I trusted Christ when I was in second grade. But I didn't follow Jesus. Yet the Spirit of God was within me, and I can look back and see His effects on my life — just like the wind. When I sinned, I felt conviction, and I felt the grieving of the Spirit. I also felt a moral restraint that kept me from rebelling too far. I watched my friends choose paths I didn't want to take, and now I look back and know it was the Spirit at work in my life. Though I was not following God closely at the time, even then I could see the wind of the Spirit blowing in my life.

As we noted in the introduction, Jesus wishes that none should perish; the one number He is concerned with is zero. Jesus said, "For God did not send his Son into the world to condemn the world, but to save the world through him" (John 3:17, NIV). Every person, apart from Christ, is spiritually dead and cannot create spiritual life. Jesus shed His blood to change that and to pave the way for us to come to the Father, and to have spiritual life. When we put our faith in Him, we receive the Holy Spirit.

The Baptism of the Holy Spirit

The *baptism* of the Spirit is different than *receiving* the Spirit. If you are a believer in Jesus, you have received the Spirit, but you have not necessarily been baptized with the Spirit. In the New Testament, the baptism of the Spirit is something that occurs to the disciples after they received the Holy Spirit in John chapter 20. It is another encounter with the Spirit of God beyond salvation.

Some people have referred to it as "a second blessing." Others, like Andrew Murray, A.B. Simpson, and A.W. Tozer, have referred to it as part of "the deeper life." Some, including Luke, call it the "filling of the Spirit" (Acts 2:4). Other places in Scripture say the Spirit "fell on them" (Acts 10:44). Sometimes the Bible says the Spirit "was poured out" (Joel 2:28; Acts 2:17). John the Baptist and Jesus refer to it as "the baptism of the Spirit" (Matthew 3:11; Acts 1:5).

I hear people argue over the terminology, and different writers throughout history have become attached to certain phrases to describe this experience. Throughout this book I will use the terms "filling of the Spirit" and "baptism of the Spirit" interchangeably. I am less concerned about what we call this, and more concerned that we are Spirit-filled people — people who live in the fullness of the Spirit of God so we can make the impact on our world the disciples made on theirs.

After Jesus breathed on the disciples in John 20:22, and said, "Receive the Holy Spirit," He began to teach them to expect a second experience with the Spirit — a fresh encounter for empowerment. In Acts 1:4-5, Jesus said, "Do not leave Jerusalem, but wait for the gift my Father promised, which you have heard me speak about. For John baptized with water, but in a few days you will be baptized with the Holy Spirit."

When Jesus used the phrase *baptized with the Spirit*, it must have conjured up images for the disciples. It would have reminded them of John the Baptist dunking people in the Jordan. Just as the people were dunked into the water, they would be dunked, drenched, soaked in the Spirit of God when they had this second encounter with the Spirit. I am sure the disciples did not know what to expect with this baptism of the Spirit, but as they waited and prayed for this gift, they must have considered the force of this image that Jesus used. I know some people are fearful of the baptism of the Spirit, but remember: Jesus called it a gift from the Father. This is something we should not fear, but eagerly long for and embrace as a gift from God.

In fact, John the Baptist declared Jesus would baptize with the Spirit from the very beginning of his ministry, and some of the disciples were followers of John and heard him say this. In Matthew 3:11, John says, "I baptize you with water for repentance. But after me comes one who is more powerful than I, whose sandals I am not worthy to carry. He will baptize you with the Holy Spirit and fire."

This prophecy of John the Baptist is fulfilled in Acts chapter 2 when the Spirit comes, and this is how Luke describes it:

> *"When the day of Pentecost came, they were all together in one place. Suddenly a sound like the blowing of a violent wind came from heaven and filled the whole house where they were sitting. They saw what seemed to be tongues of fire that separated and came to rest on each of them. All of them were filled with the Holy Spirit and began to speak in other tongues as the Spirit enabled them."* (Acts 2:1-4)

The disciples were baptized with the Spirit. They were soaked and drenched by the Spirit of God. This is not a ho-hum experience. This is something significant, dramatic, and life changing. This isn't a gentle blowing of the wind like when they received the Spirit and Jesus breathed on them; this is a hurricane force, "violent wind" from Heaven. A literal "violent wind" comes into the room as they experience this supernatural outpouring of the Spirit (Acts 2:2). This is a wind that blows and changes the landscape of their lives and ultimately the lives of countless hoards through their Spirit-saturated influence.

The baptism of the Spirit is God's ultimate purpose for His people. He didn't save us so we could go to Heaven. He saved us so He could fill us so full of Himself we could have intimacy with Him, we could become more like Him, and we could change the world with Him. We can't live the Christ-life without the Spirit's empowerment. We can't bear the fruit of Christ for the Kingdom without the Spirit's empowerment. We will never get anywhere close to zero without the supernatural empowerment of the Spirit. With the coming of the Spirit, we can now become carriers of the Kingdom because we can be filled to overflowing with His presence.

When we are living in the fullness of the Spirit, we have this sense of satisfaction, peace, and security. The life of God is poured out over our souls, and there is a sense of a supernatural sustenance deep within us. This is the fullness that can be found in the River of Life. It is the fullness of God which is a gift to His children. The best way for God to give us the gift of His fullness is to give us the gift of Himself. The fullness of God is found in the person of God, so God gives us His Spirit to dwell in us so that we can have access to the fullness of God.

The baptism of the Spirit was the turning point for the early church. They moved from a bunch of stumbling and bumbling disciples to a spiritual force that rocked the Roman Empire. They were supernaturally empowered for their mission by the great outpouring of the Spirit.

Misconceptions

I believe there are several misconceptions about the baptism of the Spirit that limit believers' expectations about the fullness they can experience. First, some argue the baptism of the Spirit was an event that occurred just for the apostles. That isn't what Peter taught. Right after the apostles were baptized with the Spirit in Acts chapter 2, Peter explains what is going on to the crowd who had gathered:

"This is what was spoken by the prophet Joel: 'In the last days, God says, I will pour out my Spirit on all people. Your sons and daughters will prophesy, your young men will see visions, your old men will dream dreams. Even on my servants, both men and women, I will pour out my Spirit in those days, and they will prophesy" (Acts 2:16-18).

Peter clearly teaches the baptism of the Spirit, this outpouring of the Spirit, is for all people — young and old; male and female; rich and poor. All people. It is the promise of God for our day and age. In Acts 2:38-39, Peter continues speaking about this outpouring of the Spirit which has occurred. He says, "And you will receive the gift of the Holy Spirit. The promise is for you and your children and for all who are far off — for all whom the Lord our God will call."

You'll notice God says He'll pour out His Spirit "in the last days" (Acts 2:16). Theologically, the "last days" began at Christ's resurrection and continue until Christ returns. We are in the last days, and God has promised to pour out His Spirit on all people. It is the gateway to the deeper life. We must have it. We must covet it.

Some have also believed the baptism of the Spirit is a one-time event. It is not — it is simply an empowering encounter with the manifest presence of God, and we can have more than one such encounter. In fact, too many people once had an encounter with the Spirit, but they are not currently living in the fullness of the Spirit. They could use a fresh encounter! I often seek God for fresh encounters, fresh fillings. Encounters help us to live in the fullness of the Spirit; they help us to dwell in the River. They fuel our passion for God.

Let's change water analogies for a moment: Think of the baptism of the Spirit like the ocean. The baptism of the Spirit should be like waves crashing up onto the shore. It is an ongoing series of events, encounters, and fillings. God doesn't just want us to be filled once. He wants us to be filled and then to live in the fullness of the Spirit.

I recalled my first encounter with the Spirit earlier, but I have experienced significant life changing encounters with God subsequent to that initial filling. I had an encounter with God in my twenties which set the direction of my ministry for my lifetime. I had another encounter with God in the midst of a marriage crisis in my early thirties that solidified God's love in my heart so firmly it led me to discover peace and security that has carried me down the River for years. I have had multiple encounters with God at the monastery where I go for spiritual retreats which have strengthened me, challenged me, and changed me. All of these encounters with God have been crucial to my River Dwelling experience.

As we continue to seek more of God, we can experience more of God. We have deeper encounters with Him. We experience Him in new ways, hear His voice to refresh us, and expand our capacity to know Him and experience His tender affections. The veil that once separated us from the Holy of Holies and His manifest presence has been torn in two, and we now have access to His presence. This is the new norm. His Spirit can be poured out again and again.

We see examples of multiple baptisms of the Spirit in Scripture. For example, in Acts chapter 2, the disciples are filled with the Spirit on the day of Pentecost. In Acts chapter 4, the same disciples are praying together. They have been threatened with persecution for preaching about Jesus, and they pray for boldness.

Acts 4:31 says, "After they prayed, the place where they were meeting was shaken. And they were all filled with the Holy Spirit and spoke the word of God boldly." They were filled again. Again, like in Acts chapter 2, the filling comes with supernatural manifestation — the room is shaken, and they spoke the word boldly. It is not a one-time encounter. The disciples experienced it more than once, and we can, as well.

After the apostles are filled a second time, there is an increase in power. Acts 5:15 records, "People brought the sick into the streets and laid them on beds and mats so that at least Peter's shadow might fall on some of them as he passed by." He only had to do "shadow healings" after being filled a second time!

Oftentimes revivals are cut short because people seek God, experience some encounter, and get satisfied. They live their whole lives looking back at their encounter with God. It's a mistake believers often make: rather than continuing to pursue more of God, we sometimes look back at our initial encounters with God, and we mistakenly think that is all there is. We need to be filled regularly, to pursue the baptism of the Spirit boldly, and to expect continuous encounters with the Living God. God is infinite, and therefore there is always more of God to be experienced.

I love studying revivals. Charles Finney was the key human player in the Second Great Awakening. Finney was a lawyer who at first was resistant to the Gospel. One day Finney went off into the woods to be alone with God. He was tired of being dissatisfied. He confessed he was a sinner and surrendered his life to Christ; it was his regeneration experience.

But later that night, Finney had a powerful encounter with God. He was baptized with the Spirit. This is how Finney described it in his own words:

"I received a mighty baptism of the Holy Spirit. Without any expectation of it, without ever having the thought in my mind that there was any such thing for me, without any memory of ever hearing the thing mentioned by any person in the world, the Holy Spirit descended upon me in a manner that seemed to go through me, body and soul. I could feel the impression, like a wave of electricity, going through and through me. Indeed it seemed to come in waves of liquid love, for I could not express it in any other way. It seemed like the very breath of God. I can remember distinctly that it seemed to fan me, like immense wings. No other words can express the wonderful love that was spread abroad in my heart. I wept aloud with joy and love. I literally bellowed out the unspeakable overflow of my heart. These waves came over me, and over me,

and over me, one after another, until I remember crying out, 'I shall die if these waves continue to pass over me.' I said, 'Lord, I cannot bear any more,' yet I had no fear of death."

This was an incredible, life-altering encounter with God. God wasn't done yet. Finney says the next day he had another encounter with God just like it. Immediately after these baptisms of the Holy Spirit, Finney began to preach, and his words had tremendous supernatural power. Finney said, "My words seemed to fasten like barbed arrows in the souls of men. They cut like a sword. They broke the heart like a hammer."

When we are walking in the fullness of the Spirit, the presence of God adds a weightiness to our words that is clearly supernatural. Our words go beyond touching the mind only and begin to penetrate the heart. Sometimes Finney noticed he was empty of this power. This is how Finney responded: "I would then set apart a day for private fasting and prayer, fearing that this power had departed from me, and would inquire anxiously after the reason of this apparent emptiness of power. After humbling myself, and crying out for help, the power would return upon me with all its freshness. This has been the experience of my life."

Finney experienced repeated baptisms of the Spirit which resulted in the presence and power of God being displayed in his life. He wasn't just filled once; he was filled and lived in the fullness of the Spirit. It is not a one-time event. We must continue to pursue more of God. That's part of the deeper life. The deeper life some of the old saints spoke of wasn't about humans cleaning up their act, it was about the life of Christ being poured out in us and leaving us marked for life and utterly transformed. It was about the deep wells of the Spirit being accessed. We need these deep wells once again.

To learn more about the baptism of the Spirit, I recommend Martyn Lloyd-Jones' book on the baptism of the Spirit, *Joy Unspeakable*. It is, in my opinion, by far the best book I have ever read on the subject. He is a well-known, highly respected, solid evangelical Biblical teacher. What I have covered here briefly, he covers exhaustively. It is a fabulous read for the one who wants to go further into this subject.

Evidences of the Baptism of the Spirit: Bold Witness

The baptism of the Spirit is a supernatural encounter with the living God that produces supernatural results. It affects our lives in significant ways. I want to look at three direct links between the Spirit's fullness and our lives. There are many indirect links to the Spirit at work in us — for example, when I was filled with the Spirit for the first time, I experienced God's love so deeply that I desired to change. Certain sin patterns were pulled up by the roots after this encounter with God. But I want to take a look at the things Scripture says will happen when the Spirit comes upon us. When the Spirit comes in fullness, there are three results, according to Scripture: bold witness, power, and prophecy.

First, the fullness of the Spirit is accompanied by a desire to witness. In Acts 1:8, Jesus said, "You will receive power when the Holy Spirit comes on you; and you will be my witnesses." One of the clear evidences of the baptism of the Spirit and the ongoing fullness of the Spirit is that we have power to witness. It is a supernatural boldness and power to witness. There is a compelling desire to tell others the Good News about Jesus along with the accompanying weightiness to our words.

The disciples spoke the word of God boldly after being baptized with the Holy Spirit. That's what happened to Peter. Before Pentecost, Peter backed down to a servant girl. He was cowardly at the cross, not at all bold. He denied Christ three times to save his own skin. After he was filled with the Spirit, we found Peter preaching boldly, even at the risk of his own life.

For example, Peter is mocked in Acts chapter 2, but he doesn't shrink back. He preaches boldly, calling people to repent of sin, and his words carry great weight — the weight of the Spirit — as people are cut to the heart and want to know how they can be saved. Three thousand were added to their number that day (Acts 2:41).

Peter is threatened in Acts chapter 4, and he tells the ones who killed Jesus that he is going to continue preaching, and he does. He is respectful and reasonable, but unmistakably bold. Once again, his words are marked with the weight of the Spirit's presence.

Even those who were threatening him took note: "When they saw the courage of Peter and John and realized that they were unschooled, ordinary men, they were astonished and they took note that these men had been with Jesus" (Acts 4:13). They could not see the Spirit, but they could see its effects — they knew something was different about these men, and they knew it wasn't their education level. It was the ongoing presence of Jesus in their lives. They had become Spirit people, filled with and walking in the fullness of the Spirit.

The leaders commanded Peter and John not to speak any more in Jesus' name, but Peter responded: "Which is right in God's eyes: to listen to you, or to him? You be the judges! As for us, we cannot help speaking about what we have seen and heard" (Acts 4:19, 20). They went right on speaking. They were filled with the Spirit, and walking in the fullness of the Spirit, and their words had great weight because of the Spirit's presence.

In Acts chapter 5, Peter was persecuted because he would not keep quiet about Jesus in spite of threats, and this is the first time persecution comes to this new Spirit-filled community. Even after being beaten, he preaches boldly. Their witness was not slowed down by the persecutions they suffered — because of the fullness of the Spirit in their lives. The beatings could not drive them out of the River, and as long as they were in the River, they witnessed with bold and weighty words.

The filling of the Spirit makes us bold witnesses. This was Finney's experience, as well. When he was filled with the Spirit, he was bold and powerful in his witness. When his witness lacked power and effectiveness, he prayed, fasted, and sought to be re-filled with the Spirit.

When we are lacking in desire and boldness to tell others about Jesus, we can make excuses, we can talk about our past experiences with God, and we can make theological arguments about how we have been filled with the Spirit. How much more effective would the church be if we simply humbled ourselves and sought God for a fresh filling until it came? How much more weight would our words have if they were marked with the present fullness of the Spirit?

When I was 19 years old and filled for the first time with the Spirit, I started making appointments with my friends to tell them about Jesus. No one told me I was supposed to do that. I had never done that before. As a matter of fact, before that encounter, I tried to change the conversation when my friends asked me what I believed. I was afraid.

After being baptized by the Spirit, I didn't take any evangelism training or apologetic courses. I was simply compelled by the Spirit's presence to tell my friends. I had the desire, and He gave me the boldness to tell others about Jesus. I didn't want any of my friends to miss out on what I had found in Jesus.

Jeff was my best friend all through my childhood. He used to hang out at my house so much my parents sometimes referred to him as their third son. He even took family vacations with us. But I never talked to Jeff about spiritual things until I was filled with the Spirit. One day I went to Jeff's workplace to see him on his break. We sat at Burger King, and I told him about Jesus, about my encounter with Him, and about His saving grace. I pleaded with Jeff to understand the Good News because I loved him, and I didn't want him to miss out. He listened intently. He didn't trust Christ that day, but it wasn't our last conversation about God. I had planted a seed, and several years later, he came to know the Lord.

After our conversation was over, an older couple came up to me and said, "Excuse me son, we heard you telling your friend about Jesus. We were praying for you. It was so good to hear a young man tell his friend so passionately about Christ."

I was experiencing the present reality of the risen Christ in my life, and I simply wanted others to know how good He was. I couldn't bear the thought of them missing out. When this compassionate desire for others to know Jesus dries up in my life, it is a sure sign that something is amiss in my relationship with God. I'm out of the River.

That is the norm for people who are filled and are currently walking in the present fullness of the Spirit. This is just what Spirit people do. They tell others the Good News of Christ. If witness isn't currently marking our lives, then let's ask God to fill us again, so we can get closer to zero!

Evidences of the Baptism of the Spirit: Power

The second mark of the baptism of the Spirit is power. Acts 1:8 says, "You will receive power when the Holy Spirit comes on you." I believe part of the power is directed toward witness. That is clear for the New Testament church. In Acts chapter 2, as we just explored, there is power to witness. They didn't witness because they were obligated to do it. They witnessed because they were compelled by the Spirit. Because they were walking in the fullness of the Spirit, their witness was powerful. Three thousand were added after their first talk — that was a powerful witness. Acts 2:47 says the Lord was adding daily to their number those who were being saved. Witness wasn't the only way the supernatural power of God was displayed in their midst. There is more to power than just witness if you take Acts seriously.

When we walk in the fullness of the Spirit, we experience empowerment for Kingdom ministry. D.L. Moody, the great evangelist and revivalist, experienced the baptism of the Spirit, and it markedly changed his ministry. Moody said he felt like he was ministering without any "unction" for four months. He wrestled with God. During those four months, God cleaned up Moody's motives for ministry. He showed him his ambition and his sin, and led him to repent.

One day Moody was in New York City walking the streets toward the house of a friend. Moody said, "God almighty seemed to come very near. I felt I must be alone." He went to the house of a friend and asked for a room so he could be alone with God. He went to his knees, and he sensed God's presence come near. Here is how Moody describes it:

"Ah, what a day. I cannot describe it. I seldom refer to it; it is almost too sacred an experience to name. Paul had an experience of which he never spoke for fourteen years. I can only say God re-

vealed Himself to me and I had such an experience of His love that I had to ask Him to stay His hand. After this I went to preaching again. The sermons were not different, I did not present any new truths, yet hundreds were converted. I would not now be placed where I was before that blessed experience if you should give me all the world."

Moody experienced the baptism of the Spirit; it changed him, and it changed his ministry. He was empowered by the Spirit. Not just gifted and called, but empowered with the supernatural power of God. Moody described it later with this image: "I was all the time tugging and carrying water, but now I have a river that carries me."

When I read the stories of great men and women who have experienced the baptism of the Spirit, my heart longs for God. Unless we have more men and women empowered from on high, we will never get close to God's sacred number of zero. Far too often we are doing ministry with human wisdom and the gifts and abilities God has given us, but without this supernatural empowerment that comes from being filled and walking in the fullness of the Spirit. Often we rely on our gifting, but not on the fresh filling of the Spirit. Sadly, it shows in the results.

The power of God is also demonstrated in Acts by other people being filled with the Spirit as the apostles minister to them. The apostles, as we've seen, are filled and refilled. Remember, it isn't just the apostles who are filled — Peter said the promise of the Spirit was for all who believe (Acts 2:38-39). The apostles experience the power of God by seeing many others filled with the Spirit in their midst.

Multiplying Spirit people is essential for closing in on zero and accomplishing Jesus' mission. People who have been filled with the Spirit, and are walking in the fullness of the Spirit, are often used by God to pray for others who need a fresh encounter with God. When their prayer is answered, God's power is displayed in the life of the hungry God-seeker.

When the apostles told the church to identify deacons for the widows in Acts chapter 6, they told them to "choose seven men from among you who are known to be full of the Spirit and wisdom" (Acts 6:3). Philip went to Samaria, and miracles and deliverances took place in his ministry there (Acts 8:6-7). Peter and John laid hands on people, and they received the Holy Spirit, too (Acts 8:17). All through Acts, people are filled with the Spirit, often through someone's prayer or preaching (as in the case of Cornelius and his household in Acts 10:44-46).

Recently I ministered in a series of special services where we were teaching on the baptism of the Spirit, and then we prayed for people to be filled or re-filled with the Spirit. We only asked people to be part of the prayer team who had been filled at one point, and were currently walking in the fullness of the Spirit. The people who were hungry for God stood to receive prayer, and these River Dwellers laid hands on people and prayed for them. Dozens of people encountered God that day in power. The baptism of the Spirit is marked with power. If we can multiply Spirit people who are empowered by God, the church can make the difference in society that Jesus intended for her to make.

Power for Healing

The power of God is also manifest when Spirit-filled people access the power of God for healing. When the present fullness of the risen Christ is active, healing often occurs. In Acts chapter 3, right after Pentecost, Peter and John meet a man who is crippled and begging. Peter commands him to rise and walk, and the man is healed.

The miracle draws a crowd. It also draws opposition from the religious leaders. The apostles are called to give an account: "Then Peter, filled with the Holy Spirit, said to them, 'Rulers and elders of the people! If we are being called to account today for an act of kindness shown to a man who was lame and are being asked how he was healed, then know this, you and all the people of Israel: It is by the name of Jesus Christ of Nazareth, whom you crucified but whom God raised from the dead, that this man stands before you healed'" (Acts 4:8-10).

Walking in the fullness of the Spirit, there is sometimes power for healing, boldness to explain it, and the eager humility to give Jesus the credit, because only Jesus can heal. Perhaps you have experienced this in your own life.

In Scripture, the apostles aren't the only ones who perform miracles. Stephen, one of the men appointed to be a deacon in Acts chapter 6, is known for supernatural power, as we see in Acts 6:8: "Now Stephen, a man full of God's grace and power, performed great wonders and signs among the people."

The very next line, sadly, is "opposition arose" (Acts 6:9). People in human power positions are often threatened by people walking in Jesus' power. The religious people began to resist the power of God, and Stephen was martyred. In the fullness of the Spirit, we see the early church operate in power for healing and boldness for witness — boldness to the death.

I didn't grow up in a church that was fluent in God's power. After I was filled with the Spirit, I began to see the Bible through new lenses. It certainly didn't make me fluent in God's power; I began to see that I had been illiterate, and I was thirsty to learn this new language.

When I became a minister, I preached about healing, and we sometimes saw people healed. Today in the church I pastor, we have seen multiple people with medically verifiable miracles. We had one man with a medical test that showed an aneurysm. A small group of people gathered around him and prayed, trusting Jesus to heal him. He went back in for another test before the scheduled surgery, and the aneurysm was gone. He asked the doctor if she would qualify this as a miracle, and she responded, "I don't see any other explanation."

In the summer of 2013, I traveled to villages in Brazil. I prayed for a young man who had a knee injury. He had limited movement in his knee along with constant pain. As I prayed, Jesus touched him. The pain disappeared, and the man's movement was restored. He ran to get his wife and brought her over to me.

The woman had a goiter on her neck. She was a thin woman, but the goiter was so large that it came out past her chin. I laid my hand on her goiter and prayed one sentence, and the goiter started to disappear under my hand. I prayed one or two more sentences, and the goiter was completely gone. The man, his wife, and I stood there in tears together, rejoicing over the present power of Jesus in our midst.

Healings are a demonstration of God's power, and we should pursue God for His healing today. We should seek His face with a theology of power, and the power will follow. I could tell many other stories of God's healing power. I am not seeing as many people healed as I would like to see, but I am seeing more than I used to see as I learn to walk in the present fullness of the Spirit.

Power of God's Love

Another way power is demonstrated is by the great outpouring of supernatural love. It is a remarkable, life-changing demonstration of power when God pours out His love in someone's heart. When the Spirit of God is poured out, we are sealed with the love of God. Romans 5:5 says, "God's love has been poured out into our hearts through the Holy Spirit, who has been given to us."

When I was filled with the Spirit, I experienced a supernatural outpouring of love. That is the dominant memory I have from my experience. Before that day, I knew God loved me theologically, but after that day, I knew God loved me experientially. I had tasted of God's great love, and it changed me.

A number of years ago, I was going to preach a sermon series on the

Holy Spirit, and I called my friend Martin Sanders. Dr. Sanders is the head of the Doctoral Program at Alliance Theological Seminary (ATS) where I teach as an adjunct professor. He and I have partnered together in various ministry settings for many years.

I said, "Martin, I want to teach on the Holy Spirit, but I would like to create a lab time after we teach on the Spirit, where we set up some experiential time for the people to experience the truths we are teaching about. We can teach about healing, and then we can pray for the sick, and as God heals, people can give testimony. We can teach about the filling of the Spirit, and then we can pray for people to be filled, and as God fills, people can give testimony."

Martin loved the idea and joined me along with Dr. Ron Walborn, the Dean of ATS and one of my dearest friends. We called it a Holy Spirit Weekend, and we hosted the first one more than a decade ago at South Shore Community Church, where I pastor. Since then, we have held Holy Spirit Weekends in many locations to help people experience renewal.

That first weekend, the three of us taught about the baptism of the Spirit, and we prayed for people to be filled with the Spirit. Many people were filled. My friend Bo McIntyre was filled with the Spirit during one of the weekends. He describes the experience in his memoir, *The Long Way Home*.

This is how Bo describes his encounter with God. He says, "I was overpowered by a blast of love so strong and overwhelming that I began to sob uncontrollably. I knew I was experiencing God's love, and that love took the form of a light so overwhelming, it was as if a thousand spotlights were switched on, illuminating every secret place in my very being. The light was so real and so bright, I was afraid to open my eyes lest it blind me. I continued to sob, but even the tears were a gift from God, for the more I cried, the more I felt a freedom, an unburdening from the pride and inhibitions that had kept me prisoner for so much of my life."

I knew Bo before his encounter with God, and I know the difference it has made in his life. He has become a tenderhearted man of the Spirit who is now sensitive to God's voice. No one can encounter the fullness of God's love without being markedly different.

This supernatural love can also lead the one who receives the Spirit's fullness to a "joy unspeakable." Peter writes in 1 Peter 1:8, "Though you have not seen him, you love him; and even though you do not see him now, you believe in him and are filled with an inexpressible and glorious joy." The disciples are filled with joy and the Holy Spirit (Acts 13:52).

Blaise Pascal is most known for being a mathematician. He was a brilliant man, not known for being overly emotional by any means. He had such an encounter with God that after he died they found him with this testimony sewn into his jacket:

> *"This day of grace 1654; from about half past ten at night, to about half after midnight, Fire. Fire. God of Abraham, God of Isaac, God of Jacob, Not of the philosophers and the wise. Security. Security. Feeling, joy, peace. God of Jesus Christ thy God shall be my God. Forgetfulness of the world and of all save God.*
> *He can be found only in the ways taught in the gospel. Greatness of the human soul. O righteous Father, the world hath not known thee, but I have known thee. Joy, joy, joy, tears of joy."*

He was filled with the Spirit and with joy unspeakable because of the outpouring of God's love in his heart.

Evidences of the Baptism of the Spirit: Prophecy

The third and final mark of the baptism of the Spirit is prophecy. Acts 1:8 reveals the first two marks of the baptism of the Spirit. When the Holy Spirit comes in fullness, we will have power, and we will witness. These are marks of the Spirit's fullness according to Jesus. There is one other mark of the Spirit's fullness which is revealed in Peter's preaching in Acts chapter 2, and again there is a direct link between the outpouring of the Spirit and prophecy.

Let's look again at Acts 2. After the apostles are filled with the Spirit, Peter explains to the crowd what just occurred:

"This is what was spoken by the prophet Joel: 'In the last days, God says, I will pour out my Spirit on all people. Your sons and daughters will prophesy, your young men will see visions, your old men will dream dreams. Even on my servants, both men and women, I will pour out my Spirit in those days, and they will prophesy'" (Acts 2:16-18).

People walking in the fullness of the Spirit hear God's voice. God said when He poured out His Spirit, people would hear from God. They prophesy — that is the Biblical word for it. Prophecy is an inspired utterance where we hear God's whispers and proclaim them to others. It is revelation from God. It doesn't come from human knowledge; we pick up wisdom, insights, and knowledge from the Spirit to minister to others. Peter said when the Spirit of God is poured out, people would prophesy. It is one of the very clear Biblical signs of the outpouring of the Spirit.

In the book of Acts, there are many examples of prophecy. For example, the Lord spoke to Ananias in a vision when the apostle Paul was converted:

"In Damascus there was a disciple named Ananias. The Lord called to him in a vision, 'Ananias!' 'Yes, Lord,' he answered. The Lord told him, 'Go to the house of Judas on Straight Street and ask for a man from Tarsus named Saul, for he is praying. In a vision he has seen a man named Ananias come and place his hands on him to restore his sight'" (Acts 9:10-12).

In this scene, Ananias gets a word from the Lord to go and see Saul (the apostle Paul). The Lord tells him the very house where Saul is located. Saul has also received a vision from the Lord that Ananias would come and lay hands on him for healing. God speaks.

Similarly, in Acts 10, Peter receives a vision from the Lord, which is another way that God speaks. The vision sets the stage for his encounter with Cornelius, the first Gentile convert.

Prophecy continues to unfold in Acts 13. Paul and Barnabas receive a prophetic word about going on a missions trip. Paul later receives a call to Macedonia in another vision (Acts 16). Paul prays for a group of disciples in Acts 19, and when he lays hands on them, "the Holy Spirit came on them, and they spoke in tongues and prophesied" (Acts 19:6). Agabus gave Paul a prophetic word that Paul would be bound and handed over to the Gentiles in Acts 21. Over and over throughout the book of Acts, people who walked in the fullness of the Spirit received communication from the Holy Spirit. They heard God speak. It is a clear mark you are living in the fullness of the Spirit.

I had never heard anyone talk about prophecy in my evangelical church growing up. It wasn't part of our experience. Sometimes people talked about promptings or leadings of the Holy Spirit, but we never would have used the word "prophecy." That was a scary word for most of those in my evangelical tradition.

But I had a grandmother who heard God speak. She wouldn't have called it prophecy either, but she knew the voice of the Lord. I remember her telling me stories that were totally compelling and could not be explained without a supernatural worldview like that in the New Testament.

For example, she told me about a time when my grandfather was away at war. He was on the Island of Iwo Jima with the Marines during WWII. My grandmother didn't know where he was, but she had this compelling urgency to pray for him. She felt a burden that wouldn't lift. She knew he was in trouble and called the pastor at her small Christian and Missionary Alliance Church and asked if they could pray together. He invited others, and by the time she arrived, a small crowd had gathered at the church to pray.

They prayed through, as old timers used to say, until the burden lifted. Later they discovered my grandfather was shot at the very hour she felt burdened to pray, and if the bullet had been just a fraction lower, it would have been a fatal shot. She and I were both convinced that those prayers saved his life. My grandmother told me many stories like that. She knew God's voice. When I was filled with the Spirit and started to hear God's promptings, I was not completely surprised, because my grandmother's stories had prepared me for this aspect of walking in the Spirit's fullness.

I will expand on this theme of prophecy in the next chapter, because the topic is worthy of exploring in much more detail. For now, it is important to note that prophecy — hearing God speak — is directly linked with the baptism of the Spirit. In the context of Acts chapter 2, Peter teaches that prophecy is for all of God's people. We can all hear Him speak, and it is a mark the Spirit has been poured out on our lives.

No doubt, some have been waiting for me to address the "evidence of tongues." I know many people have been taught the baptism of the Spirit is evidenced by tongues. Tongues is simply a spiritual language which allows people to commune with God; it is a prayer language, but it can be interpreted at times to serve as a prophetic word (1 Corinthians 14). Indeed, sometimes when people are filled with the Spirit, they speak in tongues. That happens to the apostles in Acts chapter 2 and at other times in the New Testament.

I believe in the gift of tongues, but I don't believe it is the evidence of being baptized by the Spirit. I believe it is one of the ways God displays His power when people are filled with the Spirit — that was true in Acts chapter 2. There is no place in Scripture, however, where it says, "When you are filled with the Spirit, you will speak in tongues." Nor does it say, "When the Spirit is poured out, you will speak in tongues."

The Scripture is very clear on this, though: when you are filled with the Spirit, and are walking in the present fullness of the Spirit, then you will have power, you will witness, and you will prophesy. Those are the clear and direct marks of the Spirit at work in your life.

Receiving the Baptism of the Spirit: The Pursuit

The baptism of the Spirit is something we should pursue. In Acts 1:4-5, Jesus told His disciples to wait for the gift the Father had promised. This was the "wait and pray" method of filling. It was a gift. They didn't deserve it or earn it. It was a promise they could claim, and they were instructed to wait.

Writers of old used the word "tarry." It is not a passive waiting. It is an intentional, passionate pursuit while we wait for the promise of God to be fulfilled and the answer to come. I think this is the great mistake the church makes about revival — we passively wait for God to mightily move in power, when God has told us to actively seek Him. If we seek Him with all our heart, we will find Him, the Scripture promises.

The disciples waited by passionately pursuing God for the promised outpouring of the Holy Spirit. They "all joined together constantly in prayer" (Acts 1:14). They waited in active, pursuing faith.

When you read the stories of people being filled with the Spirit, quite often there is a waiting period, where people are seeking God for a fresh filling. Moody was aware that the "unction" of the Spirit was missing. He pursued God for it, wrestled with God over it for four months, and during this time God did a deep purging. Then the filling came.

John and Charles Wesley also went through a time of seeking before the filling of the Spirit came. This is not uncommon. We have to be careful in the waiting not to grow impatient and not to take offense at God for being "slow." Allow the waiting time to prepare your heart. Allow the season of waiting to be a season of preparation, purging, and cleansing.

In Luke chapter 11, Jesus calls us to seek after the Spirit. He says, "If you then, though you are evil, know how to give good gifts to your children, how much more will your Father in heaven give the Holy Spirit to those who ask him!" (Luke 11:13). The context is about prayer. Jesus just finished telling them, "Ask and it will be given to you; seek and you will find; knock and the door will be opened to you. For everyone who asks receives; those who seek find; and to those who knock, the door will be opened" (Luke 11:9, 10).

Jesus is calling us to persist in our pursuit of more of the Spirit. In *Joy Unspeakable*, Martyn Lloyd-Jones wrote, "The fathers used to use this great term — 'pleading the promises.' You never hear it now. Why? Because people do not really pray any longer. They send little telegrams to God... They know nothing about 'wrestling' with God and 'pleading the promises.'"

Too often in pursuit of the baptism of the Spirit, people hear a story or read a chapter like this, and pursue for a little while. Nothing comes quickly, and they give up the chase. For those who would too quickly give up the pursuit, Lloyd-Jones wrote this:

> "You begin to pray and you pray really with earnestness. But you do not keep on with it, and after a while you almost forget all about it and you go back to where you were before. And you may live like that for months or years. Then again something happens and again you start — but you do not keep on, you forget. And so you go on for years, seeking spasmodically but never really receiving. . . a half-hearted, spasmodic desire is never likely to be granted

. . . there is always this element almost of desperation that comes in before God really hears this prayer and grants our request."

In our day and age, we send little text messages to God — little Twitter messages in 140 characters or less. We put in a little time, yet we want a lot of results. The reality is we need to be filled with the Spirit. We need to know how badly we need it deep within our souls. We must become unsatisfied before God will satisfy us. We must become empty before He will fill us. We must become desperate before we can be contentedly filled. It requires pursuit.

I have been preaching on the baptism of the Spirit for years. I am convinced it is the great need of the hour. I am also convinced this teaching often lies dormant during long un-revived seasons in the church, and then becomes revisited during times of revival. When we live during un-revived times, we develop theologies which fit our lack of experience and call it normal. May God help our generation to develop experiences that elevate our existence.

I have been calling people in my church to passionately pursue God for years. The outcome has been disappointing at times. In January of 2014, I asked my congregation how many of them spend 15 minutes a day four days a week alone with God. About one third of the people raised their hands. It was one of my most discouraging days as a pastor.

I have grieved it, and pressed on, but it told me a lot. And this complacency isn't just the case for lay people. I teach at seminary and recently asked a class full of pastors how many of them spend 15 minutes a day fourdays a week alone with God. The results were equally as dismal.

We know Jesus told us apart from Him we can do nothing, but we live our lives like that isn't really true. This is why far too few people are living in the current fullness of the Spirit. Imagine if I asked how many spent 15 minutes a day four days a week watching TV, or playing on social media like Facebook, Twitter, or Instagram? How many hands do you think would have gone up?

So often we wish we had more of God, but we aren't willing to pay the price. We want God to come to us on easy terms, but pursuing God is costly business. Dallas Willard said, "Grace is not opposed to effort, it is opposed to earning. Earning is an attitude. Effort is an action." We don't earn God's presence, but we do need to seek Him. We can have as much of God as we want and no more than we are willing to pay the price for. We don't get to determine when God answers our prayers of pursuit, so we must persist. The early church was continually in prayer. Jesus told us to ask, seek, and knock. There is a price to pay for more of God, but too often we aren't willing to pay the price consistently in our lives.

We need to seek God for more of Himself and gratefully receive whatever He gives. When I go away on a retreat to seek God, I am always praying for a great encounter with God, but I have resolved to be ever grateful for whatever God gives, but never satisfied — always seeking Him for more of Himself.

God has called me to battle for revival. The statistics are all going in the wrong direction when it comes to church attendance and morality, and I am in New England, where we are far ahead of this downward curve. I have realized this thing isn't going to be turned around by human effort.

We need to learn how to lead, cast vision, strategize, and execute plans better. But we need God more. With all our effort to be better leaders, we cannot afford to neglect this pursuit. We don't need a lot more human effort with a little more of the Spirit. We need a lot more of the Spirit with diligent human effort. We need Spirit-filled people. We need a fresh outpouring of the Spirit. We need the next Great Awakening in our country. The next great move of God will not be ushered in with casual pursuit. There is a price to pay.

For the past few years, I have been seeking more of God. I have been pursuing and chasing Him fervently. Sometimes I have given up food to pursue God vigorously. I've gone on longer fasts than ever before. Sometimes I have given up sleep to get up in the night to pursue God. I haven't done it begrudgingly; I have done it because I longed for more of God. I've spent more time in worship, and I've spent more time in solitude and silence. I have spent larger blocks of time alone with God — about every other month I go to a monastery to pursue God for a day or two. I am on the pursuit.

I have done these things simply because I yearn for Him. I am hungry for more of God. Remember, the River of Life is in us, and we need to dwell in the River of God's presence full-time. I don't want to get out of the River.

As I have chased more of God, I have seen an increase in the Spirit's fullness in my life. As you draw near in relationship to Him, He draws near to you. I've noticed that when I pray for people, more people are having encounters with God. More people are experiencing God's love. More people are healed. There has been an increase in power. I don't get to control it because I have nothing on my own. I have no ability to heal sick people or see prayers answered - it's God! There is a direct correlation between the presence of God flowing into my life and the answers to prayer I witness.

There has been an increase in God's presence, and with that increase I have noticed a new weightiness to my words. It doesn't have anything to do with me — I have nothing. It has everything to do with His presence.

Before Moody was filled with the Spirit, he saw a few people converted when he preached. After he was filled, hundreds of people would be converted after hearing his talks. He preached the same exact messages from the same manuscripts, but with dramatically different results. The only difference was his words carried more weight and power because of the presence of God. He was in the River of the Spirit's present fullness. He was no longer carrying water; the River was carrying him. He was filled with the Spirit and living in the fullness of the Spirit.

Can we possibly change the church today with mere human leadership? Do we really only need better methods and better programs? I am convinced the great need of this hour in history is for the people of God to be filled with the Spirit of God once again, and to live in the fullness of the Spirit. No other solution will do. Will you join the ranks of those willing to pay the price for the next great move of the Spirit?

E.M. Bounds said, "Men are God's method. The church is looking for better methods; God is looking for better men. What the church needs today is not more machinery or better, not new organizations or more and novel methods, but men who the Holy Spirit can use - men of prayer, men mighty in prayer. The Holy Spirit does not come on machinery but on men. He does not anoint plans, but men - men of prayer."

Pursuing God is costly; it is worth the price, but it is costly. The King and His Kingdom are the pearl of great price. They are worth all you have.

Receiving the Baptism of the Spirit: Receiving Prayer

In addition to waiting for the Spirit and eagerly pursuing God's presence, I also encourage you to receive prayer and the laying on of hands. Ask people to pray that you will be baptized by the Spirit.

Several times in Acts, people are filled with the Spirit when they have hands laid on them. Not everyone is filled with the laying on of hands, but many people are. Paul was filled with the Holy Spirit when Ananias laid hands on him (Acts 9:17). The Samaritans were filled with the Spirit when Peter and John laid hands on them (Acts 8:17). Apollos and his friends were filled with the Holy Spirit when Paul laid his hands on them (Acts 19:6). Notice it was all different people laying on the hands, and not all of them were apostles, but all those who laid on hands were filled with the Spirit and were walking in the fullness of the Spirit. Laying on of hands is one of the ways people are filled with the Spirit.

There is a Biblical concept of impartation. Jesus told His disciples, "Freely you have received, freely give" (Matthew 10:8). He had freely given them the gift of the Holy Spirit and His authority, and they were to freely spread the gift of His presence to others.

I love being prayed for and having people lay hands on me. When I go to conferences or when I get around people of anointing and spiritual power, I ask them to lay hands on me and to pray for me. I want more of God, and I want to walk in the Spirit's present fullness. One of the best ways I know to receive it is to humbly ask. I humble myself to receive prayer and ask God to lay it on me.

I have had people from evangelical and charismatic circles lay hands on me and pray for me over the years — people who were anointed by the Spirit and who were ministering in the Spirit's power. I've had world renown leaders pray for me, who were anointed by God and who impacted my life through their work. I've also had my friends who have been filled with the Spirit and are walking in the fullness of the Spirit lay hands on me — people like Ron Walborn, Martin Sanders, and Rich Schmidt. I've had lay people who walk in the Spirit lay hands on me and pray for me. I want as much of God as I can receive, and I'm not afraid to ask.

Ask. Have people pray over you who are walking in the fullness of the Spirit, and pray for the baptism of the Spirit.

Receiving the Baptism of the Spirit: Confession

As you are pursuing the fresh filling of the Spirit, it's important to take time to get right with God. Confess your sins to God and others. 1 John 1 calls us to walk in the light with God and others, which we will look at in more detail in chapter 4. In Isaiah 59:1, 2, the prophet says, "Surely the arm of the Lord is not too short to save, nor his ear to dull to hear. But your iniquities have separated you from your God; your sins have hidden his face from you, so that he will not hear." Our sin hinders our access to God. God has made a provision for our sin to be removed through the death of Christ on the cross, but we must confess our sin.

In Joel 2, right before the promise of the outpouring of the Spirit, there is a call to repentance: "'Even now,' declares the Lord, 'return to me with all your heart, with fasting and weeping and mourning.' Rend your heart and not your garments. Return to the Lord your God, for he is gracious and compassionate, slow to anger and abounding in love, and he relents from sending calamity" (Joel 2:12-13).

Repentance prepares the way for fresh encounters with God. Sin blocks the flow of the Spirit in our lives. We must repent from our sins, and humble ourselves and pray for the Spirit to move afresh.

Sometimes we practice what I call "sloppy holiness." We get rid of the "big" sins, but we get sloppy with "little" sins that we comfortably tolerate. We get rid of promiscuity, but hold on to some lust. We don't engage in murder, but we hold on to bitterness and gossip.

I am not a very neat person. Often times my desk is cluttered with stuff — papers, books, all sorts of things. Sometimes I put a piece of paper on my desk that I really need. I go to look for the paper, and I can't find it. I am frustrated because I need it, but I can't find it. The paper is mine. I wrote it. I need it, but I can't access it because I am sloppy. This is how it is with sloppy holiness. We have all sorts of benefits that are our privileges as followers of Christ — peace, fullness, joy, love, etc. — but often we cannot access them because we are practicing sloppy holiness.

My wife always says to me, "If you clean, you'll probably find what you are looking for on your desk." So, I start cleaning, and I throw away papers I don't need anymore, I put books on shelves, and I file the papers I do need. And usually, I find the paper. It's the same with our inheritances in Christ — as we start to repent, and clean up our sloppy sins, we begin to access the things Jesus has promised us and purchased for us.

Purity matters to God. We need to confess all sin and keep our confessions current. We need to live and die with no secret sin. This is critically important. Sin and secrets impede the work of the Spirit in our lives.

Moody experienced God's purging before he experienced God's filling. Moody wrote:

> "I believe firmly that the moment our hearts are emptied of pride and selfishness and ambition and self-seeking, and everything that is contrary to God's law, the Holy Spirit will come and fill every corner of our hearts. But if we are full of pride and conceit, ambition and self-seeking, pleasure and the world, there is no room for the Spirit of God; and I believe many a man is praying to God to fill him when he is already full with something else. Before we pray that God would fill us, I believe we ought to pray Him to empty us. There must be an emptying before there can be a filling."

Living a confessional lifestyle is a key concept in living in the fullness of the Spirit. Roy Hession's book *Calvary Road* and Norman Grubb's book *Continuous Revival* expand on this theme with great insight. I highly recommend them to you as you pursue the filling of the Spirit.

Receiving the Baptism of the Spirit: Some Final Thoughts

As we pursue the baptism of the Spirit, we need to surrender to God's sovereign choice. Jesus baptizes us with the Spirit in His way and in His time. John the Baptist said, "I baptize you with water. But one more powerful than I will come, the thongs of whose sandals I am not worthy to untie. He will baptize you with the Holy Spirit and fire" (Luke 3:16).

Jesus decides how and when we are baptized. Finney got baptized twice with the Spirit in a short time. His experiences were dramatic. He had only been a believer for a relatively few hours before he was filled.

Moody was a minister for years, and most people would have considered him successful. He felt like he needed unction, and he began to pursue. After four painful months of seeking God and emptying himself, he was filled.

As you read people's testimonies and listen to people's stories, you hear a great variety of baptism and filling stories. The Christian and Missionary Alliance has a statement about spiritual gifts — we talk about expectation without agenda. That's how we need to pursue God. We need to have expectancy, but we shouldn't demand when and how God will fill us. We can't tell Him what it should look like or feel like, or what manifestations we should or should not have. We must be surrendered. We need to be ever grateful for every good thing God gives to us but never satisfied. We need to pursue God for more of His Spirit and for an ever-deepening connection with Him. If we don't surrender the timing and the experience to God, then we will take offense. Our hearts will grow hard, and it will impede our progress. Let's trust Him, and continue to seek Him until He comes.

One last thought about how to be filled with the Spirit: step out in faith while you are waiting and pursuing. Jesus calls the disciples in Acts 1 to wait for the gift that the Father has promised. But in Mark 16, Jesus tells them to go, and the power will follow. He said to them:

> *"Go into all the world and preach the gospel to all creation. Whoever believes and is baptized will be saved, but whoever does not believe will be condemned. And these signs will accompany those who believe: In my name they will drive out demons; they will speak in new tongues; they will pick up snakes with their hands; and when they drink deadly poison, it will not hurt them at all; they will place their hands on sick people, and they will get well."* (Mark 16:15-18)

We should go in faith with the current level of the Spirit we are experiencing. Many times the Spirit will meet us while we are going on mission for Jesus. We step out in faith, often in ways that make us feel uncomfortable, and His Spirit comes in fullness as we obey. It isn't an either/or approach. We need to wait and pursue, but I also think we need to engage in the 'as you go' model of Jesus, too.

Francis Chan said, "We will never know the power of God unless we risk it all for the gospel." There is a tension between obeying God with the portion of the Spirit we are currently experiencing, and waiting for and pursuing more of the Spirit's fullness. Look for opportunities today. You may discover in the opportunities the Spirit sets before you, the Spirit's fullness awaits you.

In March of 2014 I was in an airport in Cleveland, Ohio. I was waiting to catch a flight to Erie, Pennsylvania. I was tired. It was after 11 p.m., and I had ministered in my church that day. I was headed to a weeklong speaking engagement where I would give about 20 talks and minister from morning to night over the next six days. And to make matters worse, though our plane had arrived, we had no flight crew.

I was considering renting a car and just driving to Erie. I wanted to get to bed. As I was considering this, I noticed an elderly woman who was very upset about the possible flight cancellation. She was pacing and swearing to herself. And I heard the Spirit speak, "Talk to her." I thought, "Her? Really? You want me to talk to that swearing old lady?" Right after I heard this prompting, the woman came over and sat next to me. God thinks He is so funny!

Though I was tired, I have experienced the "go and these signs will follow" movement of the Spirit in the past. I leaned into the whispers. I asked her where she was going and if Erie was home. She told me she had lived there for a long time and ran a business there. Then clear out of the blue she said to me, "What do you do for a living?"

In my line of work, that is often a conversation stopper. I knew this was a divine appointment, so I told her I was a minister. She said, "Oh, my father was a Methodist minister." We exchanged a few more pleasantries, and then our flight crew arrived and we boarded.

Who do you think I sat next to on the plane? You got it. The swearing old woman God wanted me to talk to. We were sitting across the aisle from each other, and right before the flight took off, she reached over and grabbed my arm. She leaned close to me and said, "Pray for me. I have cancer." I told her the plane was loud, but as soon as we got off the flight, I would pray for her.

We got off and she introduced me to her husband who was waiting for her. I prayed for them right in the middle of the airport in Erie at midnight. She hugged me afterwards and said, "I was so discouraged. I had nearly given up on faith. But God sent you to me today to encourage my heart."

I felt the fullness of the Spirit surging within me. I began dead tired, but now I was thoroughly invigorated with the life of the Spirit because

I had engaged in the 'as you go' model of filling. Go with what you have while you wait and pray for more.

The key to the success of the church in Acts was the baptism of the Holy Spirit. They were filled with the Spirit and walked in the fullness of the Spirit. Jesus told them one day there would be a River of Life living within them. They learned to live in the River of Life, and they ministered the life of Jesus in the power of the Spirit wherever they went. We desperately need revival today, and we need people who will not just seek God for a little while and give up. We need a Spirit-filled community of believers who will keep seeking God until He comes.

Jesus promised us we would have power, we would be His witnesses, and we would prophesy when we were baptized with the Spirit. He said the Spirit of God would flow within us like a river — He is the River of Life. We need to dwell in the River in order to access the Spirit's fullness and power. Together let's become River Dwellers, living where the fullness of God flows so we can carry Living Water to a world dying of thirst!

Reflection Questions

Chapter 1: Baptism of the Spirit

1.   Have you ever had an experience with God where you were filled with the Spirit? Describe what it was like.

2.   Are you currently living in the fullness of the Spirit?

3.   Do you see the evidences of the Spirit's fullness in your life? Are you experiencing Christ's compassion for people who do not know Jesus and a desire to tell others about Him? How is the power of God being demonstrated in your life? Are you hearing God's voice consistently? Are you developing sensitivity to the Spirit's promptings?

4.   Are you longing for more of God's Spirit, presence, and fullness? Are you willing to pay the price for more of God? How will you draw nearer to God in this next season of your life?

"I've come to believe that hearing the quiet whisper of the transcendent God is one of the most extraordinary privileges in all of my life - and potentially the most transforming dynamic in the Christian faith."

Bill Hybels, *The Power of a Whisper*

"This is what was spoken by the prophet Joel: 'In the last days, God says, I will pour out my Spirit on all people. Your sons and daughters will prophesy, your young men will see visions, your old men will dream dreams. Even on my servants, both men and women, I will pour out my Spirit in those days, and they will prophesy.'"

Acts 2:16-18

CHAPTER 2

The River Rises: Prophecy

When the Spirit of God is present, He often speaks. This is why hearing God's voice is one of the results of being baptized with the Spirit. As we develop an increased awareness and sensitivity to His presence, we become more attuned to His voice. When all of our prayer is a one-sided monologue, there isn't much depth in the relationship. In order for our relationship with God to expand, it must become a dialogue.

All of God's friends throughout the Scripture are in a dialogical relationship with Him. This is true of God's Old Testament friends like Abraham, Jacob, Moses, and Daniel. It is true of God's New Testament friends who are baptized with the Spirit and begin to hear the Spirit's promptings. It should be true of us today, as well.

After I was filled with the Spirit at 19, I started hearing God's voice fairly regularly. I didn't receive any teachings about hearing God speak. Fortunately, I recalled my Grandmother's experiences, and some of the people in my church talked about the "leadings of the Spirit." I had also read books about saints who had gone before me, like Corrie ten Boom, who talked about "direct revelation." I knew I was hearing from God.

In seminary, I discovered many of my friends and classmates had no frame of reference at all for hearing God speak. They thought God only spoke through the Bible. In spite of their skepticism, as I read the Bible, I became more and more convinced that hearing God speak was God's norm for people who are living in the fullness of the Spirit.

Let's look again at Peter's teaching on the day of Pentecost. He quotes Joel's prophecy:

"This is what was spoken by the prophet Joel: 'In the last days, God says, I will pour out my Spirit on all people. Your sons and daughters will prophesy, your young men will see visions, your old men will dream dreams. Even on my servants, both men and women, I will pour out my Spirit in those days, and they will prophesy" (Acts 2:16-18).

In the Old Testament, there were a few people who were set apart to be prophets — to hear God speak and to relay His messages. But Joel, one of God's prophets, foresaw a time where God would pour out His Spirit on all of His people, and all of His people would prophesy. It no longer would be just a select few, but there would be a community of people who were soaked in the Spirit, and one of the results of the fullness of the Spirit's presence in their lives would be prophecy. They would hear from God directly for themselves and for others. This was part of God's plan to make all of His people into a nation of priests who could bring His presence, His message, and His Kingdom to the world.

I have heard people argue that prophecy no longer exists today because of 1 Corinthians 13:8: "Where there are prophecies, they will cease." But the context explains clearly when they will cease:

> *"For we know in part and we prophesy in part, but when completeness comes, what is in part disappears. When I was a child, I talked like a child, I thought like a child, I reasoned like a child. When I became a man, I put the ways of childhood behind me. For now we see only a reflection as in a mirror; then we shall see face to face. Now I know in part; then I shall know fully, even as I am fully known."* (1 Corinthians 13:9-12)

Prophecy shall cease when we get to Heaven, and we can see Jesus face to face. In Heaven, we won't need prophecy, because we will have direct communication and direct access to God. We will be in the presence of God full-time.

Now, we only see dimly. We only hear some of what is to be revealed. We know in part. The plain meaning of the text is prophecy shall continue until we see Jesus face to face in Heaven, and then the imperfect shall disappear. We shall know fully even as we are fully known.

I have been in some church settings where prophecy is dismissed out of hand. I have been in other church settings where it has been done poorly, even recklessly. I think it is a dangerous thing to disregard or explain away a Biblical truth because some people have misused it or even abused it. John Wimber once said: The answer to abuse is not disuse; it is right use.

Fortunately, there is quite a bit of solid Biblical instruction to help us navigate our way through a wise use of prophecy. Prophecy is an evidence of the baptism of the Spirit, and listening to God's voice is a crucial part of life in the River. Let's take a look at some of those passages as we examine the three parts to prophecy: receiving a word from the Lord, interpreting the word, and delivering the word.

Receiving a Word

Paul wrote, "Do not put out the Spirit's fire. Do not treat prophecies with contempt but test them all; hold on to what is good" (1 Thessalonians 5:19-21).

When we receive a word from the Lord, it ignites the Spirit's fire in our hearts. Hearing from the Lord helps us to get into the River of Life. This is why Paul tells us not to put out the Spirit's fire and not to treat prophecy with contempt. If we treat prophecy with contempt, we risk extinguishing the flames of the Spirit. When we hear God's voice, our hearts are refreshed by the presence of the Spirit. Listening to the Spirit's promptings gives us an opportunity to have the Spirit's life renewed within us once again. We treat prophecy with contempt when we ignore God's promptings, or claim He does not speak at all.

In John chapter 10, Jesus said that His sheep would hear His voice (verse 27). Jesus goes on to teach us about the Holy Spirit in John chapters 14 through 16. He says, "The Advocate, the Holy Spirit, whom the Father will send in my name, will teach you all things and will remind you of everything I have said to you" (John 14:26).

The Holy Spirit teaches us and reminds us of the things of Jesus. He can't teach us and remind us unless He speaks to us. He is communicating to us. Jesus says, "But when he, the Spirit of truth, comes, he will guide you into all the truth. He will not speak on his own; he will speak only what he hears, and he will tell you what is yet to come. He will glorify me because it is from me that he will receive what he will make known to you" (John 16:13, 14).

Look at the words Jesus uses about the Spirit: He guides, He speaks, He tells what is to come, and He makes known. These are communication verbs. The Spirit of God communicates with the people of God. When you get to the book of Acts, this is exactly what happens. God speaks through the Spirit with His people. He speaks to apostles, and He speaks to people who are not apostles — like Ananias and Agabus. All of these things that

Jesus says the Spirit will do, He does in Acts. This direct interaction between the Spirit of God and the people of God is what makes the believers so unique. They have a relationship with God that is not dead or static or a form of religion. It is real. It is interactive. It is personal. It is intimate. God speaks.

If we are going to receive a word from the Lord, we must believe that God speaks. We must come in simple faith. God has said that He will speak to us through the Spirit, and we must take Him at His Word. We must not treat prophecy with contempt. Rather, we must learn how to hear the promptings of the Spirit.

Obviously, God speaks through the Bible, and we need to be grounded and rooted in the Scriptures. All of these prophetic promptings, these forms of direct revelation, need to be tested by what God has already said through His Word. If they are not in accord with His word, then it is not God speaking. The Word of God is inspired by the Spirit. It is our rule of faith and life. He will not tell us something by direct revelation that contradicts His Word. I also believe that there are certain depths with God that can only be plummeted through deep reflection on and understanding of the Scripture. We need to be people of the Word.

Beyond speaking to us through Scripture, God speaks to us directly through the Spirit. Let's explore six ways that God speaks directly to us. These are not necessarily the only ways God speaks, but they are listed here to help us develop sensitivity to the Spirit's voice. These are common ways God speaks to His children.

Whispers of the Spirit

First, the Spirit speaks through whispers. This is also often referred to as a prompting or leading. Bill Hybels wrote a book called *The Power of a Whisper*. It details how God speaks, and I recommend it as further reading on this topic.

Sometimes God simply guides our thoughts. For example, imagine you are driving, and all of a sudden you think of a friend. There is no reason you should be thinking of him. Nothing in particular triggered you to remember him. He just popped into your mind. You think to yourself, "I should call him." But you're driving, so you just dismiss it. The thought comes back to you, though, so you call your friend (following the cell phone laws of your state, of course!). You discover the timing was divine — at that very hour, he was in a time of need. This is a divine appointment. The Spirit guides your thoughts; it is a whisper of the Spirit.

Many of the ancient writers referred to this as "the still small voice of

God," referencing Elijah's encounter with the whisper of God in 1 Kings 19. God appeared to Elijah not in the wind, nor in the earthquake, nor in the fire, but in a gentle whisper. These promptings are easy to miss, because they are a gentle whisper, and we are a busy people.

Often the Spirit tries to reveal to us that someone is in need of prayer or a helping hand, but we are too busy to notice or too unaware that it is God gently tapping us on the shoulder. We need to become more attuned to these whispers.

One way to become attuned to these whispers is to take risks with them. If someone randomly pops into my mind, for example, I try to take a moment and pause. I ask the Lord, "Is there something you want me to do with this? Did you bring this person to my mind for a reason?" Sometimes I will get a specific answer. Other times I will have a general sense the person needs a word of encouragement. If that is the case, I will jot them a text, telling them the Lord has brought them to my mind, and I'll pass along the encouraging word. Many times I have found these little whispers turn out to be divine appointments. Following these gentle promptings is like following a pathway right to the River of Life. Continually missing these promptings can lead us away from the River, so we need to pause when they come and see if God wants us to act on them in some small way.

These promptings are often quiet — it is God's still, small voice — so you will have to take some risks. Life in the River is a life of faith. Quite often, especially as we are learning to hear Him speak, we are not sure if it is really God trying to guide us. We may hesitate because we wonder, "Is that God, or is it just me?" So we have to humbly test what we receive.

I was teaching this principle in the early days of South Shore Community Church, which I planted in October 1995 in a small town south of Boston. We only had a handful of people at the time. One night I received some devastating news; it was one of the worst nights of my life. Right after I received this devastating news, I received a phone call from the newest member of our small group, Jan.

Jan was a brand-new believer at the time. She was coming home from work, and she was praying. She got a whisper of the Holy Spirit to call me. It was about midnight. It was an incredibly risky phone call to make. She risked the hour, she risked looking like a fool, she risked being wrong, and she risked calling her pastor on a potential prompting of the Spirit. She stepped out in faith and made the call. It was one of the most memorable, timely phone calls I've ever received. I knew God knew the devastating situation and cared about what was happening in my life. The presence of God was revealed to me in the prompting that Jan received. It sealed a lesson for Jan, too. She learned God does speak, even to new believers, but she had to take a risk and obey the whisper she received. Best of all, her obedience drew both of us into the River.

Corrie ten Boom talks a lot about direct revelation in her book, *Tramp for the Lord*. She traveled the world based on God's promptings. She would wait for a direct word from the Lord about where to go next on her travels as an evangelist. Then, she would take a risk and travel to a foreign country, often without a full plan in place. Her book is a great testimony of how God can prompt His children and partner with them to advance His Kingdom if they are willing to listen humbly and follow His voice. God speaks in whispers — His still, small voice can guide your thoughts, and you need to step out in faith to humbly test what you hear.

The Audible Voice

Sometimes God speaks in an audible voice. Jesus heard the audible voice of His Father at His baptism and at His transfiguration. Paul heard the audible voice of God at his conversion. Whenever I speak to an audience about prophecy, I ask how many have heard the audible voice of God, and it is not uncommon to see one quarter of the hands go up. God speaks.

Many people have never talked about hearing God's audible voice, because they have come from a tradition where such things were not discussed. Over the years I have talked with many people who have heard the audible voice of God. Some of them are incredibly reserved people not given to charismatic experiences. I've listened to their stories, and I know the Godly effects it produced in their lives.

A number of years ago, a woman sent me an email. She attended my church occasionally when she was in the area visiting family. She was from a very traditional Congregational Church with no charismatic leanings whatsoever. She heard the voice of God, and she emailed me.

She wrote me an apologetic email with a word she had received for me. She told me she knew how busy I was, and she felt really bad about writing to me. She had been out on a walk in the woods, and she heard the audible voice of God say, "Tell Rob to write a book."

She argued with God respectfully. She told him how busy I was leading a church, teaching at seminary, raising a family, and she didn't want to tell me to write a book. She got home and told her husband, who was even more reserved and traditional than she was. He told her she had to write the email to me, because God spoke to her out loud. She reluctantly did.

What she didn't know was when I was 24 years old as a seminary student, God spoke to me about some of the things in my future. He told me I would plant a church, one day I would teach at seminary, I would travel and speak to other pastors and church leaders, and I would write books. All of those things had come true, except for writing books.

I planted South Shore Community Church when I was 30 years old, and I am approaching my 20th year as the pastor at the time of this writing. Martin Sanders taught the last class I took as a student in seminary, and I stayed in touch with him periodically over the first few years after graduating. When I was in my early thirties, he invited me to teach a class with him at seminary. I had never inquired about teaching opportunities. When he asked me, I said yes without hesitation. He said, "Do you want to pray about it?" I told him I didn't need to, because God had told me this day was coming.

In my forties, I began to get invitations to speak to pastors, and now I do travel and speak to leaders around the world. I had never sought out any of these opportunities. I just prayed and waited for God to open doors. I committed to God I would never open a door that advanced my own cause, but I would walk through any Kingdom door He opened to me for His honor. I was waiting for this door to open to write a book.

I had a file on my computer full of ideas for books I wanted to write one day, and I had been adding to it over the years. Just before this dear woman wrote to me, I started sensing a release in my spirit to write — it was an open door from God. I was praying for confirmation that He was releasing me, and that is when I received this email.

I responded and thanked her with great joy, and I explained that writing a book was something that I felt God wanted me to do, but I was waiting for His release. I told her that receiving her email was a huge confirmation. She replied with great relief and said, "Now I will tell you the rest of what God told me." She went on to say some things about my writing that are just between me and God, and they are precious to me. Given how those words came about, I have prayed about them often, and treasure them always. Immediately after she wrote that email, I started writing my first book, *Pathways to the King*.

Many Christians throughout the years have spoken about hearing God's audible voice. Joyce Meyer, for example, gives this account:

> *"I have heard the audible voice of God three or four times in my life. Two of those times were at night when I was awakened by His voice simply calling my name. All I heard was, 'Joyce,' but I knew it was God calling me...*
>
> *I heard the audible voice of God the day I was filled with the Holy Spirit in February 1976. That morning I cried out to God*

about how awful my life was, telling Him something was missing in my relationship with Him. I felt I was at the end of my rope, so to speak.

His voice seemed to fill my entire car, and He simply said, 'Joyce, I have been teaching you patience.' Since that was my first time to hear anything of that magnitude, it both thrilled and shocked me. I instinctively knew what He meant...

When I heard God's voice, I was suddenly filled with faith that He was going to do something wonderful in my life. Although I did not know what it would be, I spent the day in expectation and thanksgiving. That evening in my car, while returning home from my job, God's Spirit touched me in a special way and filled me with His presence. That event was the beginning of a new level in my relationship with God."

God speaks in an audible voice. We see it throughout Scripture, and it's not uncommon for people today to hear the audible voice of God.

Pictures — Dreams and Visions

God also speaks through pictures. Going back to Acts 2:17, Peter, quoting from Joel, said, "'In the last days,' God says, 'I will pour out my Spirit on all people. Your sons and daughters will prophesy, your young men will see visions, your old men will dream dreams.'"

God said He would communicate in pictures — dreams and visions. Dreams are pictures that come to us when we are asleep, and visions are pictures that come to us when we are awake. Not all dreams and visions are from God, but some are. We need to discern. Again, it is vitally important that we move with humility and we test everything with Scripture.

It saddens me that so many Bible-believing people scoff when I speak about dreams or visions. Some are downright mean and nasty about the topic. Yet the Bible, which they highly regard, is full of people having dreams and visions from God. Nowhere in the Bible does it say those dreams and visions will cease. As a matter of fact, in this passage in Acts 2, it actually indicates dreams and visions are part of the outpouring of the Spirit. This form of prophetic revelation is part of living life in the fullness of the Spirit. They are here to stay until the end — until Christ returns.

When we live in the present fullness of the Spirit, we will have dreams and visions. This is clearly the plain meaning of the text, and you have to do some pretty unorthodox interpretation of Scripture to come up with any other meaning.

Acts 2:17 tells us God speaks in dreams and visions. Then the book of Acts shows He did just that. God spoke to Ananias about Paul's conversion in a vision (Acts 9:10). Paul had a vision in the same passage about a man named Ananias coming to pray for him (Acts 9:12). Peter receives a vision from the Lord to prepare him for Cornelius' conversion (Acts 10). God needed to break Peter's prejudice against Gentiles, and God uses a vision which he has while he is in a trance (Acts 10:10). These aren't the only times God speaks in dreams and visions; these are just a few examples.

In the Old Testament, some prophets were called seers because they had a propensity to "hear" from God visually. They were given pictures, visions, and dreams from God. For some people today, this is the dominant way they receive from the Spirit. They get pictures.

Receiving pictures is not my primary means of hearing from God, but I do receive some pictures. They are often very quick little pictures that come to my mind and would be easy to dismiss. Like whispers, I have learned to test them humbly. I liken them to a butterfly. A butterfly often comes flitting along and lands quickly on something and then flits again — it doesn't stay in one place very long, and often these prophetic pictures come to us in the same way. When we are listening for the Spirit to speak, and a picture comes to our mind during this time of prayer, we should pay attention to the picture.

I was praying for a man one day who was trying to break free from drug addiction. He had made some progress, but he clearly had a block that was keeping him from moving forward. He was confessing some things, but he wasn't completely honest. There was a lot of shame because of all the things he had done under the influence of drugs.

As I was praying for him, I saw a picture of a white dog at the foot of the cross. I thought to myself, "that is weird." I tried to ignore it. I didn't get anything else as I waited on the Lord. I finally decided to test it. I figured there was a solid chance this was just my overactive imagination, but I wouldn't lose anything by testing it humbly.

I said, "I see a white dog at the foot of the cross. Does that mean anything to you?" The guy broke out into hysterical sobs.

I waited for him for quite some time, and eventually he confessed to bestiality. It isn't the kind of confession you want to hear, but it isn't the kind of sin someone wants to keep locked away in their soul, either. God's grace is sufficient for all of our sins, and He wanted to help that man come out of the darkness and into the light. I share this example to illustrate the awesome power of God, and how He can reach into the unknown crevices of a soul, pull out truth, and bring about healing. But the key to the breakthrough was a picture. God speaks to us to help others. It is often a prophetic word that leads someone to the River of Life.

Darkness diseases the soul, and God brings light to bear on the dark places to set the captives free. When we bring our sin into the light, light always dispels darkness. God speaks in dreams and visions, and He used a picture to bring freedom to this man.

Not all dreams are from God, as I said, but some are. How can you tell? I think there are three types of dreams. First, there are just your average, everyday dreams. These are just normal and have no significance.

Second, there are some dreams which come from our souls; they arise out of areas of our concerns. Our soul is screaming out to us, "Hey, pay attention to me down here. I am bothered, and you aren't noticing." Our subconscious pushes through to our conscious mind and brings self-aware-ness about an issue that is troubling us.

The dominant factor in these dreams is the emotion. For example, if you have a dream that is terrifying to you, you may want to take a moment and pause and pray. Reflect. Ask God, "Is there something I am afraid of that I am not paying sufficient attention to right now?" A lot of times we are ignoring our fear, and it pops up in a dream. This gives us an oppor-tunity to process the ignored emotion. These dreams are important clues to self-awareness, but they are not prophetic.

Finally, some dreams are from the Spirit. These are prophetic dreams where God is speaking to us. In the birth narrative of Jesus, for example, Joseph has multiple dreams where God communicates to him. In a dream, God told Joseph to take Mary as his wife when he was considering a divorce (Matthew 1:20). The Magi were warned in a dream not to return to Herod (Matthew 2:12). Joseph had another dream to flee from Herod and go to Egypt (Matthew 2:13). And God used a dream once more to bring Joseph and the young family back from Egypt (Matthew 2:19).

In the Old Testament, God communicates to two pagan rulers through a dream — Pharaoh and Nebuchadnezzar — and men of God, Joseph and Daniel, end up interpreting the dreams for them (see the books of Genesis and Daniel).

I have not had many prophetic dreams, but I have had some. I was teaching at Alliance Theological Seminary (ATS) well over a decade ago. I had driven from Boston to New York on a Friday night so I could get up early for an all-day Saturday class. I woke up in the middle of the night and realized I had a dream about John, a student who had been in one of my previous classes, but he was not in the current class I was teaching. In the dream he was crying. He was clearly depressed. I thought it was strange I dreamed about John, but I went back to bed.

Right before I woke up in the morning, I had another dream about

John. This time he was speaking in tongues, and he was joyful. I woke up after having these two dreams, and I simply said, "Lord, if these are from you, then let me see John when I walk into the seminary."

I walked into the seminary, and the first person I saw was John. I walked up to him and said, "Can I ask you a question?" He said, "Yes." I said, "Are you depressed?" He said, "Yes, how did you know?" I said, "It doesn't matter. Can I ask you another question? Did you speak in tongues in the past, but you stopped?" He said, "Yes. How did you know that?" I said, "That doesn't matter, but I think if you start speaking in tongues again, the depression will lift."

I had to run to class so I didn't have time to talk to him any further. I didn't see John again until three months later. He came to me and said, "You'll never believe what happened. I started speaking in tongues again, and the depression lifted." I believed it. That dream was fairly simple to interpret. Some dreams are far more complicated, and we will talk about interpretation later in this chapter.

God speaks in pictures — He promises we will see visions and dream dreams. Receiving dreams from God may not be part of your belief system, and it was not part of my church upbringing. But it is from the Bible. Don't limit the way you read the Bible by the lens of your current experience. Pay attention to your dreams and visions, and humbly ask God if they are messages from Him.

God Speaks to our Body or Emotions

God speaks through our emotions or bodies at times. Jesus said the Holy Spirit would convict the world (John 16:8). When the Holy Spirit convicts us, there is often an accompanying reaction — for example, we may feel unsettled, or uneasy, or our inner peace may be disturbed. This is part of the conviction of the Spirit. He makes us uncomfortable, and we can feel it. He isn't doing it to make us feel bad; He does it to get us back into proper alignment with Him.

It is not unlike the tension I feel when I am in conflict with someone I love. If my wife, Jen, is angry with me, for example, and she talks to me about something I have done that has hurt her, I feel uncomfortable. As I listen, own my wrongdoing, and ask for her forgiveness, then our relationship is restored. Peace returns to the relationship, and I feel inner peace again, too. I feel this same discomfort when I am out of alignment with God — it is the Spirit of God speaking to my inner being, attempting to draw me back into the River. I can't live in the River of Life while I am out of alignment with God.

The Holy Spirit also brings us peace. I'm sure there have been times in your life, like mine, when your circumstances dictated you should be a nervous wreck, but instead, you had this supernatural peace. This is a work of the Spirit of God within us. Our inner being can be at rest and calm. When we are trusting Him and walking in the fullness of the Spirit, peace is a byproduct.

Jesus is not disturbed today in Heaven. He isn't nervous, anxious, or upset. He has no challengers for His throne. No matter what you are facing, He isn't wringing His hands in Heaven trying to think about what He is going to do to bail you out. He is at perfect peace. When we are living in the fullness of His Spirit, we have His peace. The Spirit of God pours it out into our hearts — He communicates to our inner beings that all is well in spite of what we are going through.

Sometimes God gives us peace about a decision we have to make, and we take this as a green light. We interpret the peace of God as God's "yes" to this new direction in our lives. There are other times when we are going to make a decision, and we lose our peace, and we take this as a stop sign from God. God is telling us "no" about this decision. We often accept peace or the lack of peace as a way the Spirit communicates to us. It is a way He communicates through our emotions.

Sometimes the Spirit speaks through compassion. Years ago I had a dream where I was speaking at a men's retreat. As the retreat ended, I made my way out of the retreat center, and the men were coming up to me and giving me hugs. They were giving me "man hugs" — three pats and you're out. If you're a man, you're familiar with the man hug: three solid pats — pat, pat, pat — and then you disembrace, or it gets weird for most men!

In my dream, I made my way toward the exit, getting man hugs from all these guys along the way, and finally I got to the parking lot. There was one more man standing outside.

He grabbed me and hugged me like all the rest of the men. Only this guy didn't know the man hug rules. He grabbed me and held me, and held me, and held me. I could feel my skin crawling in the dream. I was squirming — just dying to get out of his arms. Then he disembraced, but still held me by the shoulders. He looked me in the eyes and said, "I am your Father in Heaven, and I love you." I collapsed into his arms and sobbed.

When I woke up, my pillow was drenched with tears. That dream changed me. I had an intimacy block with the Father for years. I connected to the Holy Spirit, because I could sense Him and hear Him. I connected with Jesus, because He was human, and I love the gospel stories about Him. The Father always felt aloof to me.

I had been praying Jesus would show me the Father, so this wall between us could be broken down. Since having this dream, I can't even mention the Father's name without feeling His tenderness. If you had asked me before that day to describe the Father, I would have said words like powerful, holy, and maybe distant. But, after that day, the first phrase which comes to my mind when you ask me to describe the Father is tender affections.

I share that story to tell you this: after I had the dream where I encountered the Father, I started experiencing the Father's compassion for people. It was very uniquely and distinctly the Father's compassion. I would walk into a room and feel the Father's compassion for someone. Often I would go up to them and tell them, "I feel the Father's compassion for you," and the person would start to cry. The Lord would give me a word for the person to encourage them. He was speaking to me first through my emotions and then with a whisper. It was the communication of His compassion that opened me up to His leading in a situation. God speaks to our hearts.

I also noticed that when the Spirit was going to give me a prophetic word to encourage someone or strengthen someone, I would oftentimes feel His compassion before the word came. I would see someone and just be suddenly flooded with a feeling of God's compassion, and I began to realize God was using this as a preemptive tactic to prepare me for a coming prophetic revelation. One day, I experienced this for a young lady, and I went up to the woman and said to her, "I have a word from the Lord for you." She said, "Tell me." I said, "It isn't here yet, but I can tell it is coming, because I can feel the Father's compassion for you." I said this to her for months. Every time I saw her, I felt the Father's compassion. I would say to her, "I still feel the Father's compassion for you. A word is coming; I can tell." She would say, "Lay it on me!" I would say, "I can't. It's not here yet. But, it's coming."

Finally, one day I went up to her with this familiar sense of the Father's compassion, and the word became clear. I said to her, "For months now the Father has given me his compassion for you, because you are about to find out something painful. He wants you to know that He knows, He has known all along, and He cares. He is with you." Later that week, she found out her husband had an affair. God had spoken to prepare her for this tragic blow.

The Spirit was speaking to me through my emotions, and I have learned to pay attention to the emotions the Spirit gives me. Now, a word of caution. Please hear me: every emotion, every dream, and every thought is not from God. They must be tested, and they must never contradict what God has plainly said in His word. Emotions in particular must be very carefully tested. We can get bent toward our desires, and then "hear God" through that idol.

For example, if we have fallen in love with someone, we might pray,

"God, do you want me to marry this person?" We can't take our strong feelings as a word from the Lord. Our strong feelings actually make it harder for us to hear from God clearly in that situation. We may be involved with someone who is not at all the right person for us, and we may have even sensed this at the beginning of the relationship, but we blew through the Spirit's whispers because our heart was bent on our own desire. We must proceed with caution. It helps to have wise and godly people around us to help us sort out what God is saying to us when our emotions are strongly involved. This is why Scripture exhorts us to "test everything."

Sometimes God can speak to us through our bodies. For example, I have had people come to me for prayer, and the presenting problem was back pain. As soon as I laid my hand on them to pray, I started feeling anxiety. I hadn't felt it before, but I started to feel it as I laid hands on them. I never just jump into prayer; rather, I take a moment to listen for the Spirit's wisdom, and sometimes that wisdom comes in the form of feeling anxiety even though I had none of my own before I started listening.

When this happens, I simply ask, "Are you experiencing anxiety or panic attacks?" I've seen many people experience freedom from anxiety through encounters like this. It is God speaking through our bodies, revealing a key which unlocks His healing power.

Our church regularly holds healing services where we teach about healing and then invite sick people to receive prayer. On several occasions, members of our prayer team have experienced pain in their bodies. For example, their shoulder began to ache. When this happened, we ask if anyone was experiencing shoulder pain, and usually someone comes forward for prayer. We have seen many healings as a result of these types of promptings. God speaks to us through our bodies, revealing His agenda for healing.

God speaks. He speaks through our bodies and our emotions, and sometimes the Spirit manifests in physical, tangible ways. Seek God, and know this is one of the ways He speaks.

A Word in our Mind's Eye

Sometimes the Spirit speaks by giving us a word in our mind's eye. We can see the word in our mind and read it. I was praying for a man one day who had back pain, and as I went to pray for him, I actually saw the word "bitterness." I could read the word as I saw it in my mind.

I asked him if there was anyone who had hurt him that he still was holding a grudge against. He talked to me about his son. His son had hurt him deeply, and he wept as he told me the story. I asked if he was willing to forgive his son. The man prayed a beautiful prayer of forgiveness through many tears; it was obviously sincere and from the heart.

By the time he finished praying, the back pain was gone. The man could bend over without any pain at all, and he was jumping for joy. His relationship with his son was being restored, and his back was healed — that is a good day in the Kingdom! These kinds of Kingdom happenings always lead me deeper into the River of Life. As that man prayed, and his back was healed, I could sense Jesus' presence with us in a strong and beautiful way.

John Wimber, in his book *Power Evangelism*, tells about a time he was flying from Chicago to New York. As he was looking around the plane, he saw a businessman sitting across the aisle from him. All of a sudden, Wimber saw the word "adultery" in his mind's eye.

Wimber was so surprised, and as he stared at the man, the man snapped, "What do you want?" A woman's name came to John's mind, and he said, "Does the name Jane mean anything to you?" The businessman replied, "We need to talk."

The plane had a small cocktail lounge on the upper level, and as the two men walked upstairs, Wimber heard the Spirit say, "Tell him if he doesn't turn from his adultery, I'm going to take him."

They reached the lounge, and the man stared suspiciously at Wimber before he asked, "Who told you that name?" Wimber blurted out, "God told me." "God told you?" The man was so shocked that he nearly shouted. Wimber said, "Yes. He also told me to tell you that unless you turn from this adulterous relationship, He is going to take your life."

The man broke. Through a choked and desperate cry he said, "What should I do?" Wimber told the man the gospel, and the man repented of his sin. Bursting into tears, he cried, "Oh God, I'm so sorry." Wimber said the man's prayer was so heart wrenching, the flight attendants were even weeping right along with him.

After his prayer, the man explained the woman he was sitting next to on the plane was his wife. Wimber told him he needed to go down and tell his wife. He not only told her his confession, and his encounter with God, but he also led her to Christ right there on the plane. That is another good day in the Kingdom! Prophecy can lead you right into the River. Sometimes God will speak by showing you a word in your mind's eye that you can read. Pay attention to those words, and test them humbly.

"The Knower"

Finally, sometimes God speaks to us directly to our "knower." This is when the Holy Spirit speaks to our spirit, and we know something we would not otherwise have known. We don't see anything or hear anything or feel anything or sense anything. All of a sudden, we just know something.

One Sunday, a woman came forward for prayer for some physical pain. She brought a little entourage with her. I had not met her or her family before, so I knew nothing about them. They just asked if I would pray for physical healing which, of course, I was willing to do.

As always, whenever I pray for someone, the first thing I do is wait on God and listen. *Theology 101: God is smart, and He knows stuff we don't know.* And sometimes, He likes to tell us what He knows. I paused to see if the Lord had anything to share, and suddenly I just knew this woman was a witch. I didn't hear anything, see anything, or sense anything; I just knew it.

Now this wasn't really a great way to start a conversation with a woman I had never met! I waited a little while longer as I prayed for a wise approach. After some time, the wisdom came and I asked her, "Can I ask you a question? Have you ever practiced any other religious practices?" She said, "I was a witch for 13 years." I said, "That would definitely count."

I went on to tell her the physical problems she had were spiritual at the root, and she needed spiritual freedom. We helped her get free from demonic issues, and God brought her some physical healing, as well. It was another good day in the Kingdom, which started from the Spirit speaking directly to my "knower."

Roger Barrier, in his book *Listening to the Voice of God,* coined this word, "knower." Barrier was headed to Denver to candidate in a church, and as he was getting ready to catch the plane, he received a call from Tucson: "We have your resume. Would you fly out and interview with our church next week?"

Barrier said while he was talking on the phone with this woman for a few moments, God spoke to him that he would pastor that church in Tucson. He hung up so he could catch his flight to Denver, but he said to his wife, "I'm going on to Denver, but God told me we're going to pastor in Tucson."

His wife Julie smiled and said, "I know. While you were talking, God told me the same thing." A week later they went to Tucson and accepted the call in a place they served for a couple of decades. People asked Barrier, "How did you know for sure Tucson was where God wanted you?" He said, "Have you ever had the experience where deep down inside you just knew what to do? . . . I call that place my 'knower.' Deep down in my 'knower,' I knew what God wanted."

God speaks. He clearly speaks through His word, and He also speaks directly to our spirit. Pay attention to whispers, pictures, and feelings you have. Pay attention to your body and to your emotions. Pay attention to the words you hear or see or sense. God promises to communicate with His children. Press in, and listen to His still, small voice. Understanding His voice and recognizing it when He speaks is important for life in the River.

Humbly Test

We've examined the various ways God speaks, and I've emphasized many times that we must humbly test what we're hearing. When we receive a Word from God — whether it be a whisper, a picture, a dream, a feeling — the first thing we need to do is test it.

1 Thessalonians 5:19-21 says, "Do not put out the Spirit's fire. Do not treat prophecies with contempt but test them all; hold on to what is good." Is what you've heard really a prompting from the Lord? How do you test it? First, test it with Scripture. If what you heard disagrees with Scripture, then it is not from God. Period. If you aren't sure if it disagrees with Scripture, then test it with others who are well versed in Scripture.

Over the years, people have told me they thought God was leading them to have a relationship with someone other than their spouse. This isn't a difficult test: it's not God. He covered that one — He spoke about it, and He hasn't changed His mind. Thou shalt not.

There are plenty of words that are not contrary to Scripture but may not be of God. For example, let's say you are praying about a job change. You aren't going to find a passage of Scripture that says you shalt not take that job. How do we test it when Scripture doesn't have a clear course of action for a specific prompting? We test it with other mature believers who are living in the fullness of the Spirit and have discernment.

I won't test words with someone who treats prophecy with contempt. They won't be able to help me. I will test words with someone who honors prophecy, and walks in humility, and has displayed discernment.

Earlier I mentioned that Corrie ten Boom traveled to different countries based on the leadings of the Spirit. She had a traveling companion with her, and together they would seek out the Lord's direction for their next trip. At one point ten Boom felt the Lord was directing her to go from Sidney to Cape Town to Tel Aviv. Her travel agent said the request was impossible, because there was no place for the plane to refuel following that path.

Ten Boom told the travel agent she must obey God: "My chief has told me I must go first to Cape Town and after that to Tel Aviv." The woman said, "Then God made a mistake. There is no direct flight from Australia to Africa since there is no island in the Indian Ocean for the plane to land and refuel. That is why you must first go over land to Tel Aviv and then to

Cape Town."

Corrie ten Boom replied, "I'll just have to pray for an island in the Indian Ocean." Then she simply prayed, "Lord if I have made a mistake in hearing your direction, please show me. But if I heard correctly, then open the way." An hour later the woman called back and said, "Did you really pray for an island in the Indian Ocean? I just received a telegram from Qantas, the Australian airline. They have just begun to use the Cocos Islands for a refueling station and beginning tomorrow will have a direct flight from Sidney to Cape Town." Corrie ten Boom trusted in God's direct guidance. She was humble; she tested it with others, and with active faith she followed the leadings of the Spirit. She lived in the River.

At South Shore Community Church, if I receive a prompting of the Spirit, I test it with other staff members and members of the board. If it is a directional decision for the church, I ask people to pray and fast with me about the issue. If we as a group don't sense the leading is from the Lord, or we don't sense that the timing is right, then we wait. There are times we have prayed and fasted together as a board and staff, and we made a decision that didn't turn out well. I think too often in the church we assume if God is leading us, then it will always turn out well, but I think that is a strange theology for a people who follow a God who died on a cross.

Jesus followed His Father's leadings to perfection, yet He suffered and died. God led many of the early followers of Christ into difficult situations. I don't think we can measure the accuracy of a leading by the outcomes of success. We must listen humbly, test it with Scripture and others, and obey God regardless of outcomes. That doesn't mean we have always gotten the promptings of the Spirit right as a leadership team. There are times we have missed them in spite of our sincere efforts to follow the leadings of the Spirit.

In Acts 21, Paul has a leading of the Spirit to go to Jerusalem. Agabus, a prophet, comes to him with a word that Paul will be handed over to the Gentiles if he goes to Jerusalem. Those with Paul, who love him, try to persuade him not to go. Paul goes anyway. Agabus was clearly right — Paul was handed over. Was Paul right to go? Were his friends right in telling him he shouldn't go? Did God lead Paul into danger? I think Paul was right, and I think God did lead him into danger. He is the God of the cross. He hasn't called us to a life of ease. He has called us to a life of obedience. Our job is to listen, test humbly, do our best to get it right, and then obey.

Interpreting the Word

After we have received a word, then we need to interpret the word.

Many mistakes in the prophetic are made during the interpretation process. We need to approach interpretation humbly, just as we must be humble about receiving a word.

If you are praying for someone and you get a prompting of the Spirit, the person you are receiving the word for should be involved in the interpretation process. Just present what you have received, and begin by asking, "Does that mean anything to you?" If there isn't a clear meaning, then wait on the Lord for wisdom. Don't elaborate on what you heard; don't expound upon it. If you receive one word, give one word and ask if it means anything. Don't give five words if you've received one.

Many people start with an authentic word from the Spirit, but then they expand on it, and by the time they finish, they have missed the moment with the Spirit. They add all kinds of human words that lack power and distract the person from what was really a little nugget from God. If they had stayed with just what God said, the person would have received from the Spirit, but often because we talk too much, the person misses the word from the Lord.

If we are going to stay in the River of Life and walk in the continuous fullness of the Spirit, we need to only give what we have received. We want to stay as close to the Spirit as we can. It will give our words more weight.

Even words that appear to be straightforward need an interpretation sometimes. For example, I was praying for a woman one Sunday at South Shore Community Church. The woman's presenting problem was a migraine headache. She was experiencing repeated, forceful migraines. I went to pray for her, and as always, I listened for any promptings the Spirit may have to offer. I felt like the whisper of the Spirit was "forgiveness."

I followed my own instructions and simply gave exactly what I had received. I said, "I think I hear the word 'forgiveness.' Does that mean anything to you?" She said, "No." I said, "Ok, let's wait some more."

But the word "forgiveness" was still the only thing I was receiving. I simply reported to her gently, "I still have the word forgiveness. Is it possible that you need to forgive someone?" She said, "I'm praying about it. But, no. I don't think so." I don't want to lay guilt or shame on someone, so I said, "It's OK. Don't worry about it. Let's wait some more."

As I waited a little longer, a thought came to my mind she was struggling to forgive herself. I said, "Could it be you are struggling to forgive yourself?" The tears started flowing, and the story came out that was the root to her shame. I don't remember if she experienced physical healing for her migraines, but the word from the Lord lightened her soul. God met her that day, and both of us were drawn deeper into the River because of the moment. Give what you receive, and wait on the Lord for interpretation.

Don't feel like you have to keep speaking; that can actually lead you and them out of the River.

I find pictures are much more difficult to interpret, whether they come from a dream or a vision. Pictures are symbolic. Scripture is full of pictures and provides us with keys to interpretation. Fire, for example, is used in many different contexts in Scripture. It can be used for judgment. It can also be used for purging, like a purifying fire. It is also used for the Holy Spirit, and the presence of God. The symbol of fire is used metaphorically for various things. The context of a symbol can help us interpret it.

Often we can interpret a dream or a vision by the way the symbols are used in Scripture. Some things, like cars, obviously won't have a symbolic interpretation from the Scriptures. But, once again, Theology 101: *God is smart, and He knows stuff we don't know.* We can ask Him to help us. You can also refer to some good books about interpreting prophetic symbols from dreams and visions.

A number of years ago I had a dream about a couple in our church. In the dream I was with this woman, and I was sad. She hugged me; we both cried and then I walked her home. But when we got to her house, it wasn't the house she currently was living in. It was a new house, and I could see all kinds of people from our church through the window.

I woke up and knew the dream was from God. Sometimes I can tell a dream is from God because it disturbs me. God often gets someone's attention through a disturbing dream. That was true for both Pharaoh and Nebuchadnezzar. They were disturbed by their dreams that were from the Lord. I prayed about the dream and had a deep sense the family was going to leave our church. I sensed they were going to take others with them, and they would be divisive. It was very sad to me.

Sometime later, it happened. Each person who was in that dream eventually left the church because of this couple's influence, just as God had warned me. Many people encouraged me to try to convince some of these people to stay. But God showed me the way things would go, and I didn't fight to protect my reputation or to keep anyone who was being influenced. I have learned to bless those who curse me, as Jesus taught. I've learned if you will obey God and do what you can do — extend forgiveness and bless those who curse you — then God will do what you cannot do: He will change your heart. And you can leave the outcomes with Him.

My heart is free from all resentment towards this couple. When I think of them, the only thing I feel is sadness — just like I did in the dream. I grieve over the loss of our relationship. The dream helped me to navigate through the difficult season, and it strengthened me through the hard time.

Interpretation is an important part of hearing from God. Ask the Spirit and other believers who are walking in the fullness of the Spirit to help you. God speaks, and, as we dwell in the River of His presence, we can start to uncover meaning behind the words, pictures, and feelings He shares with us.

Delivering the Word

When we receive words for someone else, it's important to learn how to deliver the word in a way which honors God and edifies the person. 1 Corinthians chapters 12 through 14 offer the longest teaching on prophecy in the New Testament. Paul writes in 1 Corinthians 14:1-3:

> *"Follow the way of love and eagerly desire spiritual gifts, especially the gift of prophecy. For those who speak in a tongue do not speak to other people but to God. Indeed, no one understands them; they utter mysteries by the Spirit. But those who prophesy speak to people for their strengthening, encouragement and comfort."*

Paul tells us to eagerly desire the gift of prophecy, because it is a pathway to love. 1 Corinthians 13 is "the love chapter" — Love is patient. Love is kind. Paul put it right in the middle of this teaching on spiritual gifts, because the Corinthians were trying to one-up one another with spiritual gifts.

Paul was saying spiritual gifts are a pathway to love one another, not to promote yourself. They favored tongues; they acted like if you had tongues, you had arrived at a new spiritual echelon. Paul taught that tongues are good. He mentioned that he speaks in tongues more than any of them, but he says prophecy is better, because it edifies others. It helps us to fulfill the law of love. Therefore, eagerly desire prophecy as a pathway to love others.

Prophecy is powerful when it is authentic, because when we offer someone a true word from the Lord, there is a manifestation of the Lord's presence in prophetic word. It gives them and us access to the River of Life — the Spirit of God is revealed in a true prophetic word.

1 Corinthians 12:7 reads, "Now to each one the manifestation of the Spirit is given for the common good." Paul then goes through a list of various gifts: words of wisdom, words of knowledge, faith, gifts of healing, miraculous powers, prophecy, discernment, tongues, and interpretation. These are revelatory gifts. Each time one of these gifts of the Spirit is manifest, the Lord reveals Himself. It is a revelation or manifestation of the Lord's presence. This is a powerful form of encouragement and strength to the body. This is why Paul tells us to eagerly desire spiritual gifts, especially

these revelatory gifts that manifest God's presence to people.

The purpose of prophecy is to strengthen, encourage, and comfort (1 Corinthians 14:3). Prophecy is to be motivated by love. One of the great mistakes made in the prophetic is when people give "angry" words. Anger is a powerful emotion, and it can feel very compelling. So many people assume they are compelled by the Lord to give this word, and they proceed to let someone have it, or tell it like it is. That isn't prophecy.

I was in a small group with a woman who said she had "the gift of prophecy." I actually think all of God's children can hear from the Lord (Acts 2:17), and all can prophesy. That is what Joel prophesied, and Peter claimed for us with the coming of the Spirit. Some people are clearly more adept at hearing from the Lord than others, and that's why you see some people in the New Testament who are called prophets (like Agabus). This woman, however, was often just telling people off in the name of prophecy.

I was in a small group with her for a while and had built a trusting relationship with her. One night she was telling someone she had the gift of prophecy and proceeded to lay it on the line with them. I said to her, "Can I read a passage to you?" We looked at 1 Corinthians 14:3, and I explained to her the purpose of prophecy was to strengthen, encourage, and comfort, but usually when she let someone have it, they didn't feel anything like that. I said, "I don't think this is prophecy. I think you are just angry." I was very gentle, but I was direct, and she received it. It helped her significantly. Giving angry words doesn't help anyone get into the River — not the speaker or the receiver of the message.

If you are angry with someone, don't go and tell them you feel compelled by God to tell them their mistakes. Don't blame God. We always have to wrestle with our motives. Consider these questions before giving a word: Do I want this person's best? Can I give this word in a way that strengthens, encourages, and comforts them? Is my motive to love them? If the answer is no, then don't give the word.

You may also need to consider, "Am I hurt or angry with this person?" If so, it may feel compelling, but it isn't prophecy. At that point, I encourage you to wrestle with why you are hurt or angry. Perhaps you need to have a conflict resolution conversation; perhaps you may need to forgive the person. You are not in a place to give them a prophetic word. Sometimes people use prophecy to get out of hard conversations. We don't want to do that in the name of God. The purpose of prophecy is plain: strengthen, encourage, comfort. The motive is clear: love.

Delivering a Difficult Word

While the purpose of prophecy is to strengthen, encourage, and comfort, that doesn't mean some prophetic words aren't difficult words. They can be. You can give someone a difficult, corrective word truly given in love, and it actually does strengthen the person in his or her walk with God. We just have to be careful with these, and we need to learn how to deliver them with wisdom.

If you receive a potentially difficult word, then wait on the Lord for a path to deliver it wisely. Again, make sure it isn't a word coming from hurt or anger, but it is truly from the Spirit and given in love. Wait for the Spirit to lead you into a loving pathway. If we are going to live in the River, we must live in love, because God is love.

Sometimes we are the receiver of a prophetic word, and we must test that, as well. If someone gives me a word, I always test it. Even if I don't think it is the Lord, I will test it. If it is something corrective, then I will test it with other people who are close to me, who love me, and who are not afraid to tell me the truth. Sometimes I have people who are angry with me give me a word they feel compelled to tell me, but it isn't from God at all; it is just their anger. I test it with those close to me, just to make sure I am not dismissing things I need to listen to closely. If those in my trusted circle of discerning friends agree it isn't from God, then I will "flush" it. I hold on to the good, but I don't carry the rest around with me in hurt, anger, or like a weight on my soul. I "flush" it and move on. God wants to build us up, not to tear us down.

I was teaching a Soul Care class with Martin Sanders about 10 years ago. Soul Care is a course which helps people to clean up their soul to develop a healthy inner life. They bring sins and secrets into the light with God and others. They break family sin patterns and bring God's presence to bear on some painful past experiences. They wrestle with the lies they believe, and they learn how to renew their mind. It is a very powerful week of transformation and freedom.

On the very first day of class, we got off to a late start because of a snowstorm. We decided, after a short teaching, to end the class with a model prayer time. We asked for a volunteer, and a woman raised her hand. She came up and sat on a stool. Martin and I were on either side of her, and we started simply by listening for a word from the Lord. We didn't ask her what she would like prayer for — we just listened for a prompting from the Spirit.

Martin and I were praying with our eyes open, and he looked over at me with an inquisitive look on his face as if to say, "Do you have anything?" I did, but I shook my head. He knew I didn't mean, "No, I don't have anything." But, rather, "No, I don't want to go there." He held his hands out as if to say, "Come on!" I just kept shaking my head.

The reason I was so reluctant to go there was because the word I heard was, "whore." You really want to be careful with that one! How can that be a word to comfort, encourage, and strengthen? And how can it be done in love? That's why I didn't want to go there.

As I waited on God, a question formed in my mind. I often ask for permission first, and then follow it up with a question as I explore what I am receiving. I said, "Can I ask you a question?" She nodded. I asked, "Did you live a promiscuous lifestyle at one time when you were younger?" She snorted and said, "Yes!" Immediately another question formed, "Is there a label you have for yourself as a result of those years?" She blurted out, "Whore!" and then burst into tears as deep emotional and spiritual pain came gushing out. I looked at Martin as if to say, "See! That's why I didn't want to go there!" We prayed for her, and God met that dear woman in a very special way and furthered her on the way to freedom.

Relaying the Messages of God

God wants to give us promptings of the Spirit to strengthen, comfort, and encourage people, to show He knows about them and loves them. We need to live in the present fullness of the Spirit so we can dial into His voice with sensitivity and relay these messages from God to others with great humility and compassion.

We can receive these promptings at work for coworkers, at church, in a car, or at a restaurant. Tune into them. God speaks, and living in the fullness of the Spirit involves constantly staying in tune with these promptings and delivering them in love.

We can receive these divine inspirations for believers and non-believers alike. 1 Corinthians 14:24, 25 indicates the power of a prophetic word for an unbeliever: "If an unbeliever or an inquirer comes in while everyone is prophesying, they are convicted of sin and are brought under judgment by all, as the secrets of their hearts are laid bare. They will fall down and worship God, exclaiming, 'God is really among you!'"

Sometimes the Lord will give us a specific word of knowledge we have no human way of knowing for someone who doesn't yet believe, and it will move the person's heart. Jesus has this kind of encounter with the woman at the well in John chapter 4. He gets specific knowledge about her — she was married five times before, and the man she was living with now was not her husband. It is a game changer for her, and she ends up believing because of His prophetic insight.

I told the story earlier about the woman I met in the airport in Cleveland. I have had a number of divine appointments on airplanes. It isn't an accident. I travel quite a bit these days, and when I get on a plane, I always pray, "Lord, do you want me to talk to this person who is next to me?"

Sometimes the Lord says no, and I pick up a book and read. But some of the greatest divine appointments I have experienced have been the result of prophetic promptings on a plane. You have someone sitting in close proximity to you for over an hour — it is conducive to some very cool divine appointments.

I was flying home from Pittsburgh in 2013. I was dead tired because I had been there for several days ministering at a conference from early in the morning to late at night. I got on the plane and prayed, "Lord, do you want me to talk to this woman sitting next to me?" In spite of my tired state, I sensed the Lord say yes.

She was a little younger than my mother, and I simply turned in my seat to her and started a conversation. I said, "Where are you headed?" She told me her destination. I asked her if that was home and asked about what she was doing in Pittsburgh. Very quickly the conversation went from there to spiritual things. And we ended up in a two-hour conversation about Jesus that was one of the most beautiful conversations I have ever had on a plane.

We got off the plane and she hugged me and thanked me. She said, "That was one of the most inspiring conversations of my life. It has renewed my faith." I got off the plane energized, and she got off the plane with a new desire for God. That's a good day in the Kingdom, and both of us ended up right in the middle of the River!

Preparing Ourselves to Listen: Stillness

Wouldn't it be great if every Christian were so dialed into the Holy Spirit's promptings that our lives were littered with divine appointments? Ephesians 2:10 says, "We are God's handiwork, created in Christ Jesus to do good works, which God prepared in advance for us to do."

Paul indicates God has gone before you and me this week and has set the stage for you and me to walk into divine appointments. We need to be sensitive to those; we need to allow the Holy Spirit to guide us, to speak to us, to lead us, to prompt us. We need to be full-time River Dwellers who are living in the fullness of the Spirit in this present moment so we can capitalize on every divine appointment.

How do we become more sensitive to the Spirit's voice? How do we cultivate a heart ready to hear from God? Let me end this chapter with a few practical pointers.

First, it is easier to hear God's voice on the go if we have spent time listening in stillness. If we are going to carry an inner stillness to our outer, noisy worlds, we need to create an atmosphere of outer quiet by sitting before the Lord in solitude on a regular basis. We have to cultivate sensitivity in stillness; we must be quiet before the Lord. When I have practiced hearing God's voice in the private place, I can begin to hear God's voice in the public place.

A.W. Tozer said, "The discipline of silence is the price we pay to get to know God." Psalm 46:10 says, "Be still, and know that I am God." Interestingly enough, the context is a time of trouble: "God is our refuge and strength, an ever-present help in trouble" (verse 1).

During times of stress, difficulty, busyness, and trouble, our minds speed up. We get an adrenaline rush; it is our fight or flight reflex kicking into action. The adrenaline is to help us speed up to get through the trouble and to get away from the distress. Busyness, daily troubles, and the stresses of life dull us to the Spirit's voice.

A hurried soul is not conducive to hearing the voice of God. We need to be still to recognize God's presence and activity in these chaotic times. The Psalmist does exactly the opposite thing his adrenaline rush pushes him to do. Rather than speed up, he slows down. This is the intentional disciplined action of a River Dweller. If we are going to be sensitive to God's voice in the busyness of life, then we need to develop a quiet place within our souls where we can hear God. Before we can master internal quiet in the midst of busyness that allows us to be sensitive to God's voice, we must first practice solitude and silence, and develop sensitivity to His voice in an externally quiet place.

There are places along the River journey where we are in white water rapids. The Spirit is filling us and moving us. Our lives are active and busy — this was true of Jesus. But, if we are in the River, the Spirit will always lead us to rest. There are places where the River slows down, and the water is quiet and still. If we live at a continually busy pace, we will burn out. We need these times of rest to restore our souls. In these quiet places, we restore and we still our souls, and we hear God's still small voice.

After I was filled with the Spirit and was learning to walk in the fullness of the Spirit, I started spending time each day just trying to hear God's voice. I started a prayer journal where I would write out my prayers to God, and, at the end of each time of prayer, I would spend some time listening. I would jot down what I sensed God was saying to me. I didn't take long periods of time. I often just spent five to ten minutes in silence, cultivating an awareness of His presence and listening for His promptings. This practice of becoming still before God and listening to Him each day was instrumental in helping me to begin to hear God in ministry situations and as I went throughout my day. To prepare our hearts to hear God's voice, we must carve out time to sit with Him in silence.

Preparing Ourselves to Listen: Removing Barriers

Second, if we are going to hear God's voice distinctly, we must make sure all barriers are removed. Isaiah 59:2 says, "Your iniquities have separated you from your God; your sins have hidden his face from you." Sin hides God's face from us. Sin separates us from God. We know what to do with sin — we must admit it, confess it, and repent over it. "If we confess ours sins," the Scripture says, "he is faithful and just and will forgive us our sins and purify us from all unrighteousness" (1 John 1:9). We need to make sure our confessions are current.

One of the barriers that sometimes hinders people from hearing God's voice is introspection. We get a prompting of the Spirit, but we question it. We say, "I don't know; is that God? Is that me? How can I tell?" We filter what we are receiving. We don't act on faith, and we don't risk anything.

The problem with introspection is our eyes are on us. We have to lift our eyes off of ourselves and onto Jesus. We have to repent of our pride, our self-focus, and we have to humbly receive what the Lord is saying. Start in your private time with God. Write down what you sense the Lord saying without questioning it at the time, and then test it with Scripture. We receive what He says by faith, and then we test it humbly. But sooner or later, we must be willing to act in faith. We must be willing to take a risk and act on the leadings that He offers.

A few years ago I was teaching at ATS, and we were closing class with a ministry time. There was a woman there I knew I needed to pray for. As soon as she walked in, I had this burden to pray for her. I didn't know why, but I sensed it. When we invited the class to stand if they wanted prayer, she didn't stand. So I said to Martin, "There are some more people who need prayer but haven't stood." He called again for people to stand if they needed prayer. Still, she didn't stand, but others did. I thought, "Now what?"

I still felt this compelling need to pray for this woman. I didn't know why or for what. I just knew God was telling me to pray for her. I battled with what to do for a while and finally, I just stepped out in faith. I went up to her and said, "Can I pray for you?" She was very casual and said, "Sure." With her permission, I laid my hand on her head, and she started to sob. She is a very put-together lady. This was not typical of her at all. She came up to me after class, still crying, and she said, "I didn't know I needed prayer, but when you prayed, something broke inside of me. I felt a release."

We can test what we receive humbly, but sooner or later, if the prompting is there, we have to step out in faith. Our next level with God lies outside the boundaries of our current experience. We have to risk something to get there. If we keep up our introspective question, "Is that God? Is that me? How do I know?" then we can talk our way right out of faith and miss out on what God is doing.

Sometimes we are hindered from hearing God clearly because of the "bent will." Our will gets bent toward our desires, and the thing we are bent toward we will hear from like an idol.

For example, imagine someone named Sue struggles with people pleasing. Underneath people pleasing is a fear of not being loved or a fear of rejection. Sue has a close friend who is headed down a path that could lead to significant soul damage, and Sue senses that the Lord wants her to intervene. Sue wants to help her friend, but she is terrified of having this difficult conversation, because she wants her friend to be pleased with her. She prays, "Lord, do you want me to talk to my friend?" Because her will is bent by fear toward people pleasing, she can't hear from the Lord. She filters what the Lord is saying through the idol of people pleasing, and she doesn't intervene. This is the bent will.

When our will is bent, we have a very difficult time sorting out God's voice from our own desires, because our will is bent toward the object of our desire — whether that is pleasing people, financial gain, or some illicit relationship. This is why I have had people come to me and say, "God told me to leave my wife and marry this other person." No, He didn't. This is a classic case of the bent will. We must surrender our will to God and God alone. We must be willing for His desires for our life, and be willing to give up all but His will. We must get unbent toward idols, and bow our stiff neck to God alone. Only then will we hear His voice clearly.

Preparing Ourselves to Listen: Becoming Aware of His Presence

Finally, we want to become conscious of God's presence. He is with us always, but we need to intentionally turn our attention to Him. It is in the River that we are most attuned to His voice. Hebrews 12:2 says we should fix our eyes on Jesus. I often come into His presence with thanksgiving and praise. Psalm 100:4 says, "Enter his gates with thanksgiving and his courts with praise; give thanks to him and praise his name." Thanksgiving and worship pave the way into God's presence.

In the Old Testament, some of the prophets would worship in order to prepare to hear God's word. We see this in 1 Chronicles 25:1, 3: "David, together with the commanders of the army, set apart some of the sons of Asaph, Heman and Jeduthun for the ministry of prophesying, accompanied by harps, lyres and cymbals . . . Jeduthun, who prophesied, using the harp in thanking and praising the Lord."

Worship can prepare our hearts to hear God's word, because it draws us near to God's presence. Sometimes just taking a walk in nature can heighten our awareness to God's presence and prepare our hearts to hear God.

Many people have experienced prophecy done poorly and are reluctant to venture into this realm. I have had people give me words without any humility at all. I have had others tell me off because they were angry, and call it prophecy. I have seen people give "words" that were not of God at all, but simply human stuff that they wanted to say. I've also had people like Jan call me with a word from the Lord at a critical moment in my life, and it ministered His presence deep in my soul. The right answer to misuse is not disuse — it is right use. Prophecy is Biblical, and Scripture has given us wisdom about how to do it well.

If we are going to become people of the Spirit, we are going to have to learn how to hear God's voice. God speaks. He speaks in whispers and pictures; He speaks in emotions and in words and straight to our "knower." He speaks to us so we can build up others — so we can strengthen, encourage, and comfort others in love. When we are tuned into His voice, we are dwelling in the River and living in the fullness of the Spirit. Prophetic words can lead us and others into the River of Life.

Reflection Questions

Chapter 2: Prophecy

1. In what ways have you heard the Spirit's promptings (audible voice, whisper, dreams and visions, a word in your mind's eye, or just knowing)?

2. What is the way you are most comfortable receiving from the Lord? Is there one way you tend to hear most often?

3. Have you ever missed a prompting of the Spirit? Recall that. Why didn't you act on it?

4. Do you regularly take time to be still and listen?

5. Is there any "static" in your life that needs to be removed? Is there any sin that needs to be confessed or hurried sickness that needs to be addressed?

6. Consider starting a listening journal. You may even open up a file on your smart phone. Take a moment to quiet your soul right now, and listen. Jot down what you sense the Father may be saying to you. Humbly test it.

7. If you are in a small group, take a moment to listen to the Spirit for one another. Give only what you receive. Humbly test it. Be sure to give the word in love to strengthen, comfort, and encourage.

"The world is perishing for lack of the knowledge of God and the Church is famishing for want of His Presence. The instant cure of most of our religious ills would be to enter the Presence in spiritual experience, to become suddenly aware that we are in God and that God is in us."

A.W. Tozer, *The Pursuit of God*

Jesus said, "Let anyone who is thirsty come to me and drink. Whoever believes in me, as Scripture has said, rivers of living water will flow from within them."

John 7: 37, 38

CHAPTER 3

Living in the River

As I write this in June 2014, my wife, Jen, and I are about to celebrate our 24th wedding anniversary. I love being with Jen. Over the past few years, we've had some really fun travel experiences. We have been to foreign countries together, like England, Brazil, and Spain. We have been on some great excursions throughout the United States, including cities in New York, California, and several states along the east coast. I love being able to take these trips, explore new places, and visit historic sites. Traveling has been a fun and exciting way for us to build memories together.

I also love the conversations we've shared. Over the years, Jen and I have had some incredible conversations where we shared from the heart, talked about deep things, navigated parental challenges, or had profound conversations about God and things of faith. These have been life-giving dialogues.

I don't need to visit new places or have a life-changing conversation with Jen to enjoy her company; I am equally happy just to take a walk with Jen in our neighborhood, hold hands, and chat. We don't have to do anything or say anything. I just want to be with her.

This is true of my relationship with God, also. I have had some memorable experiences with God over the years — they have been relationally deepening, life-altering experiences. I also love just to sit in quiet and be with Him. I have come to covet His presence above all things in my life.

Like my relationship with Jen, I just like to be with Him. I don't have to be doing anything for Him or saying anything to Him. I don't have to be reading the Bible or worshiping. I just want to be in His presence, and I want to stay in His presence as much as possible.

I have had various encounters with God over the years which have been like great trips. They are refreshing and full of great memories. I love having these mountaintop experiences with God. They have marked me. I have often heard God's voice, and it has shaped me. My post pivotal life change moments all involved God speaking to me; He revealed Himself to me in some way. I've discovered most life change occurs alone with God. It is hard to authentically encounter the living God and remain as you were. I covet these encounters with Him, the memories they create, and the ways they have shaped my life.

But my question at age 19, after my first life-changing encounter with God, is still the most pressing question: How do I stay there, in the fullness of God's presence? How do I live in continuous renewal? That's what we'll discuss in this chapter — how to continually dwell in the River.

The Longing of our Soul

Christianity is first and foremost a passionate love affair with a once blood-stained and now risen Savior. In the book of Revelation, we learn the church at Ephesus lost their first love, and Jesus addresses them because of it. They are commended for being a good church. They were a solid church and didn't have any sin that Jesus addressed. They were grounded doctrinally. They withstood evil. The only thing Jesus reproaches them for is that they had lost their first love. They weren't deep into sin or false beliefs; they had simply lost their passion. They once had it, but they couldn't sustain it. They had gotten out of the River, and Jesus calls them back.

The truth is, it is easy to drift and lose our way. Spiritual complacency is common in comfortable societies. There are so many things to distract us, and so many things our hearts can become attached to. We cannot live in the River with a heart that has become attracted to many things and is distracted from our first love. We must learn how to dwell in the River full-time so we don't end up losing our passion, like the church at Ephesus.

In John 7:37, 38, Jesus said, "Let anyone who is thirsty come to me and drink. Whoever believes in me, as Scripture has said, rivers of living water will flow from within them." There is a hunger in every heart, a thirst in every soul, which only God can fill.

David felt this deep hunger for God. He wrote in Psalm 63, "You, God, are my God, earnestly I seek you; I thirst for you, my whole being longs for you" (verse 1). In every soul, there is a greedy, eager, restless longing only God can satisfy. It's as if there is a hole in our soul, and we need it filled.

We often turn to things other than God out of this ravenous longing. Some people try to fill up this hole in their soul with success, money, or material possessions. When we first buy something new, it gives us an emotional boost. You buy a new car, and you feel a thrill when you first drive it. The first few times you get in and smell the new car smell, it is satisfying. But that feeling doesn't last; it doesn't satisfy for long. The new car smell goes away. Some guy at the grocery store carelessly dings your door. Soon the new becomes old, and the empty feeling starts surfacing again.

Others try to fill this deep longing with pleasure. They turn to lust or sexual exploits, or drugs or alcohol, to fill the void. Sex is good, but the good feelings don't last, and we crave more. The soul constantly cries out for more. It is never satisfied.

This is why people become addicted to things. They keep returning to the empty and broken cistern hoping to find living water there that will satisfy their deep longings. They end up ensnared — ever thirsty, but never satisfied. We try to borrow life from things which cannot give life. Good things often point us to the source of life, but they have no life in and of themselves. This is why there is a restlessness in our souls. Only God satisfies.

David turned these inner desires toward God. His longing motivated his pursuit of God's presence. He writes later in the Psalm it is God's love that satisfies, so "my soul clings to you" (Psalm 63:8, NIV). We must learn to go to God for satisfaction and to rest in His presence. In the River of His presence, there is a continuous flow of His life in our inner being. This is the only place that can satisfy the deepest longings of our soul.

Many people confuse doing religious activities with experiencing God's presence. They aren't the same. We can read our Bible and never encounter God. The Pharisees did that. We can pray and yet not meet God in prayer. We can go to church and never change. I know many people who have sat through church services over the years. They sang the songs and listened to the sermons and volunteered in various ways, and all the while they lived a double life. They engaged in religious activities, but they didn't meet God.

Religious activities, which don't lead to soul-satisfying drinks from the fount of Living Water, will never quench our spiritual thirst. We will only fully be satisfied, completely devoid of the longing, when we see Him face to face. Only then, in His fully revealed presence, will our satisfaction be lasting and complete. But even now, we can drink deep of the Living Water and find satisfaction moment by moment. The Living Water is the Spirit of

God, which Jesus promised would flow from within us. If we dwell in the River, He will be enough for us day by day.

The Living Water

The Israelites in the Old Testament struggled to follow God. If you read the story, you will see that they constantly wandered off into sin, rebellion, and idolatry. Jeremiah the prophet records these words from God: "My people have committed two sins: They have forsaken me, the spring of living water, and have dug their own cisterns, broken cisterns that cannot hold water" (Jeremiah 2:13).

Rather than coming to the Living Water to satisfy their souls, they kept running to other wells that could not satisfy the deep longing of their souls. The water God offered them was a spring; it was continually flowing with fresh, clean water. They rejected Living Water and dug their own cisterns instead. These cisterns had no source of water that could continually be replenished, like the spring. The water in them was not fresh or flowing. It was stale, stagnant water. Worse yet, their cisterns were broken so the water couldn't even be held within them.   They constantly searched, yet were never satisfied, and always frustrated, yet never turned to the Source of Living Water. God continually sent them leaders and prophets to call them to repent. Sometimes they repented for a while, but it never lasted long, and they would go back to their old rebellious and idolatrous ways. They returned once again to their broken cisterns.

So God promised them a new covenant. Not a covenant marked by the blood of animals, but a covenant marked by the blood of His Son. Not a covenant marked by the law, but a covenant marked by His Spirit living within His people, flowing the Living Water over their hearts.

The Lord said through Ezekiel, "I will sprinkle clean water on you, and you will be clean; I will cleanse you from all your impurities and from all your idols. I will give you a new heart and put a new spirit in you; I will remove from you your heart of stone and give you a heart of flesh. And I will put my Spirit in you and move you to follow my decrees and be careful to keep my laws" (Ezekiel 36:25-27). They couldn't keep the covenant, so God was going to give them a new heart and put His Spirit in them. This was the promise of a new covenant, a new birth, a new life.

At the end of Ezekiel, the prophet receives a vision of water flowing from the temple. The water kept flowing and getting deeper and deeper, until finally it became a river Ezekiel could not cross.

The Lord tells Ezekiel, "Where the river flows everything will live" (Ezekiel 47:9). It is the River of Life. Jesus connected these Old Testament prophecies to the coming of the Holy Spirit. He becomes in us that River of Life. It is only in the River we can have the rest and satisfaction our souls crave. It is only in the River our eager, greedy, restless souls can finally find their satisfaction. We need God; our souls covet His presence. Rather than laboring hard to carry water from broken cisterns, we can now come to the springs of the Spirit where fresh water can flow continually over our souls.

The Spirit gives us continual access to the presence of God. God is the author and source of life. If we can stay in the presence, if we can stay in the River, we can live in continuous renewal. *Where the river flows everything will live.*

When I had my filling of the Spirit as a young man, people told me it was just a mountaintop experience, and I wouldn't stay on the mountaintop. They told me to expect the feelings, even the closeness, to fade. They were essentially telling me I couldn't dwell in the River. I could visit it from time to time, but they warned I was unable to stay there.

But Jesus promised us the Spirit would dwell within us like a river. We don't have to make our homes deep in the woods, occasionally making an excursion down to the River so we can lug water back to camp. We don't have to live in the camp, continually fearful we will run out of water with a mindset that says, "Beware. There isn't enough." The River flows, and everyone who dwells in the River can access the continuous life of God that is found there. In the River, there is fullness. There is continuous renewal for those who dwell there, and we must learn to dwell there full-time.

Cultivating God's Presence

If we are going to become full-time River Dwellers, then we must cultivate God's presence. Let's think about the presence of God in three ways. There is the omnipresence of God. God is always present: all times, all places, and all seasons. David says in Psalm 139:7-10, "Where can I go from your Spirit? Where can I flee from your presence? If I go up to the heavens, you are there; if I make my bed in the depths, you are there. If I rise on the wings of the dawn, if I settle on the far side of the sea, even there your hand will guide me, your right hand will hold me fast."

We know this is true, but we are not always aware of His presence. God was present when you woke up this morning, and showered, and ate your breakfast, and drove your car, and interacted with the people in your life. He is present with us when we are at church, and when we are watching TV. He is with us when we are engaged in our most sacrificial loving act, and when we are in self-absorbed sinful behavior. However, many people go through their daily life without any thought about God, even though

He is there. The omnipresence of God is comforting, but it does not satisfy the eager, greedy restless longing of our souls.

Then there is the manifest presence of God. There is a big difference between God's omnipresence and His manifest presence. Sometimes His presence is manifested; it is revealed or made known. The manifest presence of God cannot be missed. It can be misunderstood and mislabeled, and it often is, but it will always be noticed.

Think of the story of Elijah at Mt. Carmel in 1 Kings 18. God was present the whole time. He was present when Ahab and Jezebel were killing the prophets, but no one knew He was present. He was there when the prophets' blood flowed, because He is omnipresent. He was present with Elijah in hiding, but Elijah might not have always been keenly aware of that fact.

There was a marked difference between the omnipresence of God throughout Ahab's reign and the manifest presence of God as the people watched the showdown between Elijah and the prophets of Baal. God asked Elijah to call the people of God together for a definitive moment when the people could see which god was God. The prophets of Baal came to represent the god Baal. There were 400 of them. Elijah stood alone on the Lord's side. Both sides cut up a sacrifice. Both sides built an altar. Both sides laid the sacrifice on the altar.

Neither side lit the fire for the sacrifice. The rules of engagement were the true God was to light the fire. The prophets of Baal got first shot. They prayed. They cried out. They cut themselves. Blood flowed, but fire did not fall from the heavens. When it was Elijah's turn, he couldn't help himself — he upped the ante. He poured water over his sacrifice and altar. He wasn't a showoff. He just wanted the people to know who was God. Elijah then prayed a simple, faith-filled prayer, and fire fell, proving that the God of Israel, Yahweh, was the true God.

When the prophets of Baal called out to their gods, the people were not aware of God's omnipresence. They sat by passively like a bunch of people in church and watched the show. Then Elijah prayed, and the fire fell from Heaven and licked up the sacrifice, the water, and the stones. The people became keenly aware of the presence of God. His presence was manifest, and it was not possible to miss His appearance: "When all the people saw this, they fell prostrate and cried, 'The Lord — he is God! The Lord — he is God!'" (1 Kings 18:39).

God showed up in power — in visible and tangible ways. There was no mistaking His presence now. It was a fall-on-your-face-and-cry-out-to-God presence. It was a "God is God, and there is no other" moment. God was there the whole time, but then there was a moment in time when God revealed Himself — His presence was manifest. That's a whole different experience.

Think about Moses. God was always present in the times of Moses. But sometimes God manifested His presence with Moses, like at the burning bush, or on Mt. Sinai, when the mountain was covered in smoke and fire, and the earth trembled in the presence of God, and God spoke. God was present with Moses before the bush started on fire, but He was present in a visible way in that bush and when He spoke. It changed Moses. God was present in the camp of the Israelites before the cloud descended on Mt. Sinai and the fire, smoke, lightening, and thunder came. When the cloud descended on the mountain, it was a visible manifestation of God's presence that was frightening to all.

In the New Testament, Paul reminds us we are transformed by the presence of God. In 2 Corinthians 3:17-18, Paul writes, "Now the Lord is the Spirit, and where the Spirit of the Lord is, there is freedom. And we, who with unveiled faces all reflect the Lord's glory, are being transformed into his likeness with ever-increasing glory, which comes from the Lord, who is the Spirit."

In this context, Paul was talking about Moses. As Moses went into the presence of God, his countenance would glow from the reflection of God's glory. It was like the moon reflecting the light of the sun. The moon has no light in itself; it can only reflect the sunlight. If the sun stops shining, the moon stops glowing. Moses glowed with God's presence. The manifest presence of God marked him. It changed him and had a visible effect on him, and the people could tell.

The glow on Moses' face would fade, so he would put a veil on his face. It would fade because Moses didn't have continual access to the presence of God. He could come into God's presence on the mountaintop, but he couldn't stay there — so he would put the veil over his face so the people couldn't see the reflection of God's presence fading.

Paul says we are different — we are not like Moses, because we do have continual access to the presence of God. Not just His omnipresence, like Moses always had, but we have continual access to His presence in a new way, because of the Spirit of God within us. He is a stream of Living Water, and we can live in the continual stream of the presence of God (John 7:37). When we intentionally cultivate the presence of God, and live more and more in the stream of His presence, we are transformed.

The third way I would like us to think about the presence of God is this sense of His cultivated presence. The manifest presence of God satisfies our souls. But we can't make God manifest His presence. We can pursue Him, but we cannot produce the manifest presence of God. Now the Spirit lives within us, and we can always cultivate His presence. Cultivating God's presence is not manufacturing a sense of God's presence, or pretending it's there. Instead, we intentionally develop an awareness of the presence of God — an awareness which allows us to drink of the Living Water and find satisfaction for our souls, an awareness allowing us to stay in the flow of the Spirit.

When a follower of Jesus "practices the presence of God," as Brother Lawrence described it, there is a developed awareness of God's continual presence. We can learn to find the stream of Living Water, and we can dwell there. We can learn to find God wherever life finds us. There is often a low-level manifestation of His presence in this developed awareness. There may be a sense of His peace as the River of the Spirit runs through us. Sometimes the River will produce a continuous knowledge of the love of God poured out into our hearts (Romans 5). It can produce a joy or contentment. At times His presence may come with a visceral reaction — a slight trembling, a tingling, or some other sense of the Spirit's presence with us. We can learn to recognize God's presence as we go through our day, and we can learn to be aware of Him. Our souls can find rest in His presence.

Practicing the presence of God is learning to become more attentive to your spiritual senses. If you were walking outside in the woods, there would be animals and birds all around you, but you may not be aware of them. You may not be able to tell the different sounds that each bird makes. You may pass by a bird and not even register its song. But if you began to study the birds in your area, and became a student of their habits, behaviors, and sounds, suddenly you would be very aware of the birds around you. You would hear the different birdcalls. You would know what to look for, what to listen for, and how to pay attention.

Nothing in the woods has changed. The woods are the same as they were before, but you have changed. You have become attentive to the reality of the birds in the woods. It is the same with practicing the presence of God; we learn to become attentive to the presence of God within us in a new way. We don't miss His presence like we did in the past.

Jesus was a master at attuning to His Father's presence. This is why throughout the gospel of John He says things like, I only go where the Father tells me to go, I only say what the Father tells me to say, I only do what the Father tells me to do. He was constantly aware of His Father's presence and leadings. He was completely dialed in.

Practicing the presence of God is also about availing ourselves to God in such a way that we become attuned to His presence. God is omnipresent. He is always here, and sometimes His presence is manifest. As River Dwellers, we must cultivate an awareness of His presence as we dwell in the living stream He offers. I think there may be times in our life where God has manifested His presence to us, but we missed it because we were unaware of His presence — just like Moses when he first saw the bush, just like the person walking through the woods but unaware of the birds around him. Cultivating God's presence can make us miss these divine interactions less frequently and help us to dwell in the River more consistently.

Recognizing God's Presence

How do we develop this cultivated awareness of God's presence that flows within us like a stream of living water? First, we must begin to recognize what the presence of God is like in our lives. Sometimes the manifest presence of God comes in ways very loud and clear and can't be missed — though they can be mistaken for something else, and often are.

When God visits Mount Carmel in 1 Kings 18, His presence was not subtle! The presence of God in the burning bush was much more subtle. Moses didn't know God was visiting him until he approached the bush, and God spoke. God's presence is visibly manifest in both instances. When we practice the presence of God, we have to learn God's ways of visiting us. I think there are times when God is visiting us, but we miss it because we fail to recognize how God reveals His presence.

God visited Moses and the Israelites in Exodus chapter 19, and there was thunder, lightning, and smoke. God spoke, and He descended to the top of the mountain. That was not subtle.

The still, small voice of God spoken to Elijah in 1 Kings 19 was not what Elijah expected. He would have been less surprised to find God in the wind, the fire, or the earthquake — especially right on the heels of the Mt. Carmel showdown where God demonstrated His presence in powerful ways. But He came in a still, small voice. God's presence comes subtly at times and other times with great force. We have to learn how to recognize God's presence however He chooses to come to us.

There have been times in my life where God has spoken to me, and it was loud and clear. It was supernatural in every way, and life altering. Some of these occasions have marked me and my spiritual journey. They were not subtle. But there are many more occasions where God has spoken to me in a still, small voice. It was simply a quiet whisper. It was much easier to recognize God's presence when He came in a thunderclap experience than when He came in a whisper — that was true in the Old Testament, and it is true today for us. We have to lean into these subtle expressions of God's presence if we are going to live consistently in the presence of God.

Most of us have experienced the presence of God manifesting within us as deep peace, even when circumstances dictated we should not feel peaceful. Most of us have experienced some level of God's love being poured out in our hearts or revealed to us in a personal way. We have felt His compassion in a time of pain, or His mercy being poured out after we repented, or just a keen sense of an awareness of His love that came by revelation of the Spirit. Many of us have known of God's love intellectually because we grew up in the church and heard the message of Jesus' love for us many times, but then one day we knew God loved us deeply and personally. The Spirit of God made it known to us somehow, someway, and this love we had heard about and believed became real. It was revelation. God visited us.

Many times the Spirit comes to us with a wave of compassion for someone else. We may mistake this for our affections for a person. We think, "Oh, I love Sue. She is so sweet." Sometimes that wave of love we feel is a gentle and subtle manifestation of the Spirit. He may be calling us to minister to Sue, and we need to tune into those emotions.

Many of us have experienced a gentle touch from the Spirit that resulted in joy — a sweet joy that was a clear touch from the Spirit. Many of us have woken up one day with a fresh sense of His mercies being new that morning, and it filled us with joy. Nothing in our circumstances had changed, but God was there making Himself known to us in a fresh way. These are all signs the Spirit of God is visiting us. He is drawing us to the River, but we must recognize it for what it is, and welcome His approach. We must step into the River of His presence in these moments. The more often we recognize them and live into them with God-awareness, the more consistently we will live in the River. Cultivating a continuous awareness of God's presence can help us catch these gentle winds of the Spirit.

Manifestations of God's Presence

Sometimes there are significant manifestations of God's presence. Sometimes when the Spirit comes upon someone, there is a bodily reaction; the person has a visible manifestation of the Spirit's presence. In Acts 13:52, we read "the disciples were filled with joy and with the Holy Spirit." The fullness of the Spirit led to an overflow of joy in their life.

Sometimes the overflow of joy may lead someone to laugh. Some have called this "holy laughter." Others have mocked it. I was with a group of believers who were talking about a revival that had received some press. One of the things it received press about was this phenomenon of holy laughter.

The group all stood around and scoffed and mocked the reports of holy laughter. Though I have not experienced holy laughter personally, and at the time of the conversation I had not witnessed it, I had studied revivals, and I knew this rendition of holy laughter was not the first appearance it had made in history.

I said to them, "Do you think the revivals under John Wesley and Jonathan Edwards were authentic?" They said, "Yes, of course." I explained they had experienced holy laughter in that revival. They didn't call it holy laughter, but they described the phenomenon. They also experienced it in the Second Great Awakening. John "Praying" Hyde, the great missionary to India, talked about holy laughter, as well. In his autobiography, Billy Graham actually mentions laughing for joy when he was filled with the Spirit after being prayed for by Stephen Olford. Holy laughter has appeared over and over again on the pages of history. It can be a manifestation of the Spirit.

Another manifestation can be seen when people fall under the weight of God's presence. In the early days of my denomination, the Christian and Missionary Alliance, they called it "prostration." Paul King, in his book *Genuine Gold*, records many examples of people falling in prostration under the weight of the Spirit's presence in the early days of the Christian and Missionary Alliance. Some people call it being "slain in the Spirit." My friend Martin Sanders is fond of calling it "carpet time."

I know a whole bunch of people would just dismiss these manifestations, but I would urge you to be careful. There are Biblical examples of people falling down under the weight of God's presence, the most prevalent example being John the apostle. He was the one who laid his head on Jesus' breast, but in the book of Revelation, he encounters the risen Christ and he testifies, "When I saw him, I fell at his feet as though dead" (Revelation 1:17). Sounds like some carpet time to me. I don't want to miss God's presence because I dismiss a manifestation that is outside of my experience and my comfort zone.

I was recently ministering at a Holy Spirit Weekend in New York. God was moving in unusual ways that particular afternoon. Many people fell down under the weight of God's presence as we prayed. After more than a dozen people had experienced this weighty presence of God, I went to pray for a man named Bill to be filled with the Spirit.

Bill is a big guy, and as I was about to pray for him, a young woman named Jenn stood behind him, ready to catch him if he fell. I looked at her as if to say, "Are you sure you want to try to catch him?" He caught my expression and turned to her and said, "That's all right; I won't need anyone to catch me. I'm not going down."

I simply laid my hand on Bill gently, and within five seconds, he fell down (she didn't do so well catching him, but he landed softly enough). As he fell, he just laid on the ground and laughed, deep from the gut. He laughed and laughed. It truly was holy. The presence of God was there, and Bill was filled with the Spirit and with joy — just like the disciples. I laughed with him and prayed, "Give him more, God! He's a big man; he needs more. Fill him up!" He laughed with gales of laughter filled with the joy of the Spirit's presence. When was the last time you were so filled with God you just laughed for joy?

People may also tremble or shake as a manifestation of God's presence. I was praying for my wife one day and she began to shake. Her jaw began to tremble. My wife is as authentic and honest a person as you will meet. She would never fake anything, nor would she ever do anything to draw attention to herself. It was just God. This is how He chose to come to her and make Himself known on that occasion.

You may ask, "Why would God shake Jen?" I'll give you three reasons. First, because what the Spirit of God mostly wants is full access to us. He wants control of our lives. He wants to be the leader. He wants us to completely trust Him and follow Him by faith. That means we can't have, and won't have, everything figured out and put into a neat, tidy theological box. Sadly, many times people revere their theological systems more than they revere God's presence. That was true of the Pharisees, and they ended up missing God in their midst.

Second, because Jen has often struggled to connect with God, and has even felt a little forgotten at times. This was a clear way for God to say He noticed her, had not forgotten her, and was with her. It was undeniable.

Third, Theology 301: *God is weird, and He does stuff that we cannot understand, and sometimes He doesn't care to explain Himself.* I say this with absolute reverence and no disrespect. He is different. Read the Bible: it's full of weird experiences.

In Ezekiel 4, God commands the prophet to lie on his left side for 390 days, then lie on his right side for 40 days. God tells him to cook his meals on human excrement (Ezekiel 4:12). Ezekiel protests the last one, and he talks God into cooking it on cow dung instead. Personally, I might have tried to talk God into letting me cook on rotten wood, but no matter how you cut it, this isn't an average every day conversation with God that Ezekiel is having! In chapter 5 he had to shave his beard and his head. This is all a little weird, and this only covers one prophet and two chapters.

Sometimes God comes to us in ways which don't make sense to us. God may visit someone with holy laughter, and someone else may tremble in His presence, and someone else may speak in tongues. Sometimes when God fills people with the Spirit, they have this tremendous encounter with the love of God flowing abundantly in their souls. That is the testimony of many who have had filling encounters with God.

I don't believe we should seek manifestations, but neither do I believe we should dismiss them or fear them. When we have Holy Spirit Weekends, we often see manifestations. We don't promote them. We don't encourage them or seek them. Many times the people who experience manifestations have never experienced them before. When God comes in power, things happen. Don't seek manifestations. Seek the Master. But don't resist manifestations, either. You don't want to resist a manifestation and find out you were resisting the presence of God.

Most of the people I pray for don't experience great manifestations; they experience a gentle sense of God's presence, a touch of His love, a sense of His peace. It is also easy for some people to be disappointed they didn't get a greater experience. I don't think we should compare our experiences with others. We should be ever grateful for however God chooses to reveal Himself to us, and yet never satisfied. We should continually pursue Him for more of Himself. Let's make God our pursuit, and not His gifts nor His manifestations.

Testing Manifestations

Just as we need to test words humbly, we should also test manifestations. Not everything is from God, but just because it is outside of your experience, doesn't mean it is from the evil one, either. Sometimes manifestations are from God, sometimes they are human, and sometimes they are demonic. I have prayed for people and seen manifestations for all three of those reasons. They need to be tested by spiritually discerning people.

Martin Sanders and I were teaching a class once, and a woman fell over. I knew right away this fall was demonic. Just as the Spirit can manifest, so too can demons manifest. As I approached her, I just knew it in my spirit — it was one of those "knowing" encounters with God's voice. I said to Martin, "It's demonic." He said, "How do you know?" He was still trying to discern. I said, "Watch."

I knelt down and whispered one word to the woman: "Jesus." She started growling. We discerned rightly it was demonic, and we helped her get free.

I've also experienced manifestations that occur because of human emotion. A prayer line formed during a special service we were holding, and as I walked down the line, I prayed for people. I didn't pray anything audibly; I just laid hands on people as I was in the presence of Jesus. The first person I prayed for fell to the ground, and shortly after, she started weeping. It was grief. It was neither God nor demonic; it was just a person collapsing under the weight of grief. We assigned a couple of prayer people just to sit with her and quietly pray for her while she grieved.

I was in another class shortly after that, and I prayed for a woman who fell over. I knew this was clearly the Lord's presence, so I let her lay there on the ground, and I went to pray for someone else. Another woman in the class was visibly upset because she had never seen anyone come under the weighty presence of God before. She was saying this couldn't be of God. My friend Ron Walborn says that oftentimes we confuse our comfort zone with discernment. When something is outside of our comfort zone, we say it can't be God and call it "discernment." Just because we have never experienced something before doesn't mean that it isn't God. The Pharisees used that logic to say that Jesus was operating by the power of the enemy.

Martin knew that this woman was experiencing God's presence, but he called me over and asked me to help. I knelt down and whispered one word to this woman on the floor: "Jesus." She said, "He is so sweet. So beautiful." I said to her, "What are you experiencing?" She said, "Perfect peace. Deep love. Healing love. Jesus' presence."

As she said these words, the presence of Jesus was so palpable in the room this other skeptical woman who was there started to cry. She knew it was God, and we all witnessed a powerful, life-changing encounter with the manifest presence of God.

Manifestations happen. Sometimes people shake a little. Sometimes people laugh as they are filled with the Spirit. Sometimes people cry, even loudly, as the Spirit convicts them or heals a deep wound within them. Sometimes people fall under the weight of God's presence. Of course, sometimes people take a courtesy fall; it's just a learned behavior from their religious culture. We need to have spiritually discerning, River Dwelling believers who can rightly discern the presence of God. Manifestations can happen. Don't seek the manifestations; seek the Lord.

The Presence

Cultivating a sense of God's presence is about developing spiritual sensitivity to the Holy Spirit's activity in our lives. When I am in the presence of the Spirit, I can often feel Him viscerally, but it is far more subtle than holy laughter or some other manifestations. I have cultivated God's presence over many years and sometimes I can feel His presence, for a lack of a better description, like a rushing wind inside me. Most of the time, no matter where I am, I can simply pause, fix the eyes of my heart on Jesus, and sense the Spirit within me. I love His presence, and I want to become more and more sensitive to it. We can't expect this sensitivity to the Spirit to come to us suddenly. It is consciously developed over time.

It is like a marriage relationship. When Jen and I first got married, I would offend her with things I said, and I wouldn't even realize it. I wasn't able to pick up on her social cues and her subtle facial expressions of hurt. I still miss too many of those sorts of things, but I am far more sensitive to my wife than ever before. When my words hurt my wife's feelings, I am often cut to the heart.

This is what happens when people grow closer over time — they become more tender with one another, more sensitive to one another, more alert to each other's heart. This is how it should be with our relationship with God. As our spirit is linked closer to His Spirit, we move in rhythm with Him, and when we get out of rhythm, we feel the grief caused to His Spirit. We know what the River feels like, we know when we are in the River, and we know when we have left it.

In Brother Lawrence's book, *The Practice of the Presence of God*, he describes how he has tried to live his entire life in the conscious awareness of God's presence. It was his ambition not just to experience God's presence in the sanctuary, or in prayer, or in worship, but to experience God wherever he was, whatever he did. He tried to keep his mind on the Spirit's presence throughout his day. He began to heighten his sensitivity to the presence of God so he could be aware of God in the sanctuary and in the kitchen peeling potatoes.

Being attuned to God's presence is almost like someone who has lost one of their senses, like sight. They heighten the other senses, like hearing. I heard of one blind person who was able to tell different types of trees by the sound the wind made blowing through their leaves. It had never occurred to me wind would make a different sound blowing through different leaves. I have the same ability as that man to hear with such sensitivity, but I have never developed the capacity to hear with such clarity. We all have that capacity, but our senses are often not sharpened enough to use it. It is the same with our spiritual sensitivity. We must develop it, sharpen it, and heighten it.

Developing spiritual sensitivity is directly connected to being aware of God's presence. Intentionally focus on God's presence, discover what His presence is like in your life, and fix your attention onto Him.

Spiritual Disciplines

If we are going to access God's presence with greater sensitivity, we must engage in spiritual disciplines that get us to the River. Spiritual disciplines are not an end in themselves; they are a means to an end. The disciplines are a tool to help us get to know God and access His presence. The purpose of reading the Bible is not to know your Bible. The purpose of reading your Bible is to know God. When we treat the discipline as an end in itself, we miss out on the presence of God. We become religious rather than River Dwellers. Engage in disciplines that feed your soul and increase your awareness of the Lord's presence. Everyone is wired differently. You will discover there are certain disciplines that are very meaningful to you, and you should press into those disciplines.

Gary Thomas wrote *Sacred Pathways*. He talks about some different pathways to connect with God. It is an excellent book. When I grew up in the church, there were only two disciplines anyone talked about: read your Bible, and pray. What we meant by read your Bible was start left in Genesis and go right until you hit Revelation, and then do it again. I did that for years.

I still read through my Bible because I gain some benefit from it. But I discovered it wasn't my best avenue of connecting with God in Scripture, so I have added other approaches to Bible reading over the years — like praying Scripture, meditating on Scripture, and studying Scripture.

When we talked about prayer, we mostly were speaking about intercession. I intercede for people — it is part of our priestly function as believers. But again, it isn't my greatest connection point with God through prayer. For many years, I engaged in Bible reading and prayer, but I wasn't dwelling in the life-giving River; it wasn't helping me to cultivate an awareness of God's presence. It is easy to confuse religious activities for River Dwelling. They aren't the same thing.

I was thirsty, and those disciplines were not connecting me to the Living Water. If going to church, reading your Bible, and praying don't heighten your sensitivity to God's presence, then your soul will remain irrepressibly dry. We must commit to spiritual disciplines that get us in the River.

Meditating on Scripture

We need to engage in disciplines which allow us to access the River. There are many books about spiritual disciplines, and so I don't need to elaborate on all of the spiritual practices here. I'll give you some of my life-giving spiritual practices, not because they are right for you, but as a parallel learning opportunity.

Meditating on Scripture is one spiritual practice that can increase our awareness of God's presence. 2 Timothy 3:16, 17 says, "All Scripture is God-breathed and is useful for teaching, rebuking, correcting and training in righteousness, so that the man of God may be thoroughly equipped for every good work."

God didn't just breathe on the Scriptures when He inspired the authors to write it. Every time you pick up the Bible, you are one Holy Spirit breath away from a God encounter, from a life-giving interaction with the Author of Life. He is present in His Word. He can reveal Himself to you as you slowly and carefully read that inspired text with an expectation to catch the breath of the Spirit.

When we read the Bible, we need to pay attention to those moments when the Holy Spirit is breathing on a passage. Often a word will jump out at us, or a phrase or an image will grab us. Something that we are reading will catch in our spirit, and that is a time to pause. This is the time when the Spirit is visiting us in that moment, and if we are going to become River Dwellers, we cannot pass these moments by. As we pause where the Spirit breathes, we are increasing our sensitivity to His presence. This practice will carry with us into other moments in life when the Spirit is revealing himself to us. Too often we are trying to get our reading done so we can check it off our list, and we press on to finish our allotted chapters. When we do that, we miss the Holy Spirit's breath in our life. I have read too many chapters of Scripture while bypassing too many breaths of God. I am learning to cultivate His presence when I read the Scripture, and to catch those Holy Spirit breath moments.

If you are reading a chapter, and a verse or a phrase catches in your spirit, pause there. Linger with it. As you sense that stirring of the Spirit, ask the Spirit to give you wisdom, revelation, and insight. Ask Him why this is grabbing you. What is He trying to reveal to you? Why is that phrase or image stirring something inside of you? When we are sensitive to the presence of God as we read the Scripture, we don't just check off our Bible reading, we meet with God. We get into the River.

This morning I was alone with God, and I read Psalm 62. I never made it past verse 1: "For God alone my soul waits in silence; from Him comes my salvation" (ESV). There are certain things I am confronting in my life right now I cannot resolve. I need God. I cannot fix them. I cannot alter my circumstances; they are beyond me. This phrase grabbed my soul, and I have lingered with it in silence for much of the day. The Spirit was breathing on it, and His presence was peacefully manifested in my life as I meditated on that revelation about God.

Worship and Thanksgiving

We can enter God's presence through worship and thanksgiving (Psalm

100). On Sundays, it is often hard for me to enter fully into the worship experience. I have a talk to give and things to do. But during the week, I will pull out my iPhone (which is loaded with worship music) and engage in personal, private worship alone with God. It is one of my favorite ways to draw near to the presence of God.

I stumbled upon private worship years ago, when worship cassettes first came out. I was worshiping alone with God one day, and tears just streamed down my cheeks as I was ushered into His presence. I was surprised by the presence of God in worship.

As I worshiped, I suddenly found myself standing right in the middle of the River of Life. The Spirit's life and love poured over me. I love to engage in personal and private worship, but I have discovered I need to change the music often. When I can sing a song, and it no longer affects my heart, it is time for me to purchase new music. If I can sing, and think about something else, then I need fresh worship music. I often will worship to a new album for a couple of months, and then I need something fresh — it has to touch my heart or it no longer draws me to the River. It's a discipline that connects me to God's presence, and you may find it connects you with the Living God, as well.

Praying Scripture

I mentioned meditating on Scripture, but I also love praying Scripture. I often will pray the Psalms. Today I meditated on Psalm 62, and I prayed it back to God. I will often read through some Psalms until I find one that particularly resonates with my own life situation. I will pray that back to God with my own words, reflecting through my own life circumstances.

The Psalmists are raw. They process deep pain. The Hebrews were very good at processing pain and grieving — unlike us Americans who tend to numb pain. We medicate it with pleasure or busyness or Facebook or pharmaceuticals. We hate pain and try to eliminate it at nearly any cost. The Hebrews processed pain; it was just part of life, and they found God in the midst of it. Praying the Psalms helps me to process the honest and raw emotions of life and to access the presence of God.

David and the other Psalmists always end up with trust. In the end, after they process life's painful places, and wrestle with God, they surrender. Some people never process their pain, and their eager, greedy, restless souls long for something to fill the void — the result is often an attempted drink from a broken cistern. Some people get stuck in the pain and never leave the grieving. The discipline of praying Scriptures, especially the Psalms, has helped me to process my emotions, surrender my heart to God, and get into the River of Life.

Solitude and Silence

Solitude and silence have been key disciplines for me to connect with God and thereby develop increased awareness of His presence. In my book *Pathways to the King*, I talked about taking ten-minute retreats. These are brief breaks in the day where I pause and fix my attention once again on Jesus. They are brief moments in time where I recalibrate my heart heavenward. They get me focused on God's presence again. They get me back in the River. Most of the time when I take a ten-minute retreat, I sit in silence alone with God. I may start by meditating on a verse of Scripture the Spirit breathed on earlier in my time with God. I am intentionally pausing my busy day to be in His presence. This pause not only allows me to adjust and get back into the River, but it allows me to move through my next sequence of events with greater awareness of the Spirit.

If I retreat with God frequently, I can live in His presence with more consistency. Oftentimes, I just sit in silence in His presence. As I mentioned in the beginning of the chapter, I love to be with Jen. I don't always need to be talking with Jen to enjoy her presence. In the nice weather, we just take a quiet walk and hold hands. The little stroll in the evening is refreshing for me, because Jen's presence is refreshing in my life.

Those little walks also help me to get into the River, because nature has a way of drawing my attention to God. In my relationship with God, I need these little reminders of His presence. God's presence is restorative. It is refreshing. *Where the River flows everything lives.* I try to take ten-minute retreats where I simply fix the eyes of my heart on Jesus. I intentionally slow down, refocus on His presence with me, and I get back in the River. I don't say anything or pray anything. I just sit with my Savior, or go for a quiet stroll with Him through nature, and notice His goodness. If we are going to consistently spot the hand of God in our lives, we must cultivate a quiet, unhurried soul in a noisy, busy world.

Busyness can mask the soul's emptiness for a season, but eventually the soul's poverty is somehow revealed. God calls us out of our busyness into divine inactivity. It isn't sloth. It is purposeful inactivity where we attune to His presence and enter His rest. Human inactivity is often escapism. It can be lazy and a time waster. Divine inactivity is restful, reparative, and restorative. When our lives are hectic without enough purposeful divine inactivity, we will run from activity to escapist behaviors. These escapist behaviors are quick "feel good" acts, but they do not lead to restoration. They cannot bring the rest of the Spirit's presence.

We must choose rest that can be offered in the presence of God through silence, solitude, and stillness. I have discovered the more outputs my soul produces, the more stillness I require to replenish and grow. The busier I become, the more I need to embrace divine inactivity where I can once again cultivate His presence and rest my soul.

Listening Prayer

Listening prayer is another discipline that allows me to enter into God's presence. Prophecy, as we looked at, is a manifestation of God's presence (1 Corinthians 12:7-11). When God speaks, God reveals Himself. I practice listening prayer on a regular basis, and when God speaks, it is like a cup of Living Water quenching the thirst in my soul.

Often when I listen in prayer, the Lord simply reminds me that He loves me. Everyone desires to be loved, and love is refreshing. Christianity is, first and foremost, a passionate love affair. God wants to tell you that He loves you. He has told you in the Scripture, and He reveals it to your heart through the Spirit. Romans 5:5 says, "God has poured out his love into our hearts by the Holy Spirit, whom he has given us." Listening to the Spirit reveal the Father's love helps me consciously walk in the presence of God.

Find the disciplines that feed your soul, and engage in them. I want to encourage you to take a moment and journal right now. What disciplines do you need to engage in to keep your soul fresh? How often do you need to engage in them? I had to develop a rhythm of spiritual activities I could engage in so I could stay in the River, and I have had to adjust it over the years. Often when I hit a spiritual plateau, it is because my rhythm is no longer working, and I need to adjust it. There are certain spiritual practices I engage in daily, weekly, monthly, and yearly so that I can sustain my spiritual well-being. Do you know what your spiritual rhythm is? Are you engaging in a rhythm that is keeping you spiritually refreshed? If not, what do you need to do differently? Ask the Holy Spirit for wisdom, if you aren't sure. Theology 101: *God is smart, and He knows stuff we don't know.* And sometimes, He likes to tell us what He knows. After you have established a rhythm, you need to periodically evaluate it. Is it working? Is it keeping you in the River?

As you develop your rhythm, I encourage you to try many disciplines. Richard Foster's book, *Celebration of Discipline,* is an excellent resource for exploring the spiritual disciplines. Many people have found it helpful to include disciplines that you are not attracted to naturally. I would not naturally choose silence, but it has become one of the most meaningful disciplines in my life. It has helped me to surrender more fully to God and to experience a deeper peace — especially when life is hard. In silence, I give up all control and just sit and wait in the Lord's presence for the Lord's deliverance. Broaden your experiences. If I had limited my spiritual practices to those I had been exposed to in my youth, I would have lived most of my life on the riverbanks.

Make spending time with God a non-negotiable in your life. Put God on your calendar. I made a decision to spend regular time with God nearly 30 years ago, and that regular, consistent time with God has made all the difference in my life. I have changed the disciplines I engage in over the years. I have adjusted my spiritual rhythm as needed. I've adjusted what spiritual practices I engage in and the frequency with which I practice them. I have never gone back on my fundamental commitment to be with God. I committed to do whatever I needed to do to stay fresh with God and live consistently connected with Him. When I feel like I am losing ground spiritually, I make an appointment to get alone with God. When I feel like I am out of the River and onto the banks, I make an appointment to get alone with God. I do whatever it takes to get back in the River. Spending time alone with God is a life commitment every serious River Dweller must make.

Recognizing Spiritual Hunger

Another thing that can greatly increase our sensitivity to God's presence is to recognize how often we misdiagnose spiritual hunger. Our spiritual hunger is a gift from God to draw us into the River, but far too often we don't recognize this hunger as a spiritual tap on the shoulder by the Spirit of God. I'll give you the classic example. Let's say you finished eating dinner at 6:00. You cleaned up the dishes, put away the food, and you go into the living room to sit down. You are checking email, looking at Facebook, watching TV, or reading a book. After a little while you think, "I need a little something."

You wander back into the kitchen to satisfy this desire for "a little something." You aren't hungry; you just ate. So what is that desire? It isn't a physical desire for food. I think quite often we are feeling spiritual desire; we are longing for God. We are misdiagnosing a spiritual hunger, and because we feel an emptiness inside, we are associating it with physical hunger. It is the empty, eager, greedy, restless longing of our soul for something more. It is our soul longing for God — the only One who can truly satisfy. The Spirit of God is triggering our heart longing, so that we will come to Him. It is a sign of His presence; it is an invitation to His companionship.

Often we misdiagnose these spiritual desires, and we try to fill our spiritual hunger with a physical solution. Those physical solutions actually dull the spiritual hunger in our lives. We reach for a snack, and we anesthetize our spiritual longing for God. So we need to identify and pay attention to these spiritual longings.

If we are going to stop dulling our spiritual hunger with material things, then we have to become aware of what we run to when we are spiritually hungry. Some people run to sinful things — things like drinking too much, drugs, pornography. Those things are pretty obvious red flags that we are not living in the River.

But a lot of times we don't run to sinful things. Some of us run to busyness. We check email. We get productive. We clean up. We pick up a professional journal. We fight off our emptiness with busyness.

Some people run to other people — we go to our friends, or to our cyber friends on Twitter, Facebook, and Instagram. Sometimes we run to food. Sometimes we run to shopping. We often run to these things so frequently when the hunger strikes that we become addicted to these things and sadly, they never satisfy. They are broken cisterns. We run to them, nonetheless, because we hate the feeling of emptiness that often accompanies our longing. We are afraid to feel that empty feeling, so we seek to fill it. Most of the time, we are not even conscious of why we are doing it; it has become a reflexive response to our inner longings.

When we are feeling a spiritual longing and we run to some physical answer, we are running from the River of Life. The Spirit is calling us to Himself, and we are moving away from the River. What are the things that dull your spiritual hunger? Discover and eliminate those activities.

I'm not saying that we should never go on Facebook, never be with friends, or never go for dessert. Actually, we can be with friends and eat dessert with a conscious awareness God is giving us these pleasurable gifts as a sign of His goodness, and we can draw near to Him in that moment. I am not saying we must always abstain from pleasure. I am saying we need to recognize the things we run to when the desire for God strikes, and we need to understand how running to those things can sometimes lead us away from the awareness of God's presence.

What are the things which compete with the Spirit's call to draw near? When spiritual hunger strikes, go to God. Embrace that empty feeling, and run to the River of Life where everything lives.

Spiritual Desire

Rather than dulling our spiritual longing, we need to intentionally cultivate spiritual desire. We need to feed our spiritual hunger. It is like throwing logs on a fire. If we want our fire for God to burn hot, we must continue to throw logs on the fire. If we don't feed the fire, the fire dies down. Cultivating spiritual desire feeds our fire for God. It helps us to increase our desire and our awareness of His presence; it leads us to the River.

Recently, a young woman came up to me after a church service. It was only her second time at our church. She said, "I've been here twice now, and both times I just cried through the service." I've had this same conversation with dozens of different people over the years. I asked her, "Do you know why you cried?" She said, "I don't know. I'm not sad." I smiled and said, "No. I don't think you are sad. It's God's presence. You sense His presence, and it is tapping a deep longing in your heart. You long for God."

As I said this to her, tears filled her eyes. We long for God, and if we are going to practice His presence and draw near to Him, we need to cultivate this longing and not dull it.

David was masterful at managing his spiritual longings and maximizing their spiritual fruitfulness. I mentioned Psalm 63 earlier, and let's look at it closer. David writes, "O God, you are my God, earnestly I seek you; my soul thirsts for you, my body longs for you, in a dry and weary land where there is no water. I have seen you in the sanctuary and beheld your power and your glory... On my bed I remember you; I think of you through the watches of the night" (Psalm 63:1-2,6).

David feels this intense longing for God. It feels like a gnawing emptiness in his soul. He identifies it and recognizes it as a deep soul thirst. He doesn't seek to numb it or dull it. He embraces it, and he directs it Godward. That's the key! We must direct our spiritual longings Godward. We need to see the longing as a gift from God designed to draw us near to God. We must embrace it and lean into it.

David says his soul thirsts for God, and his body longs for God like a desert land without water. He realizes the longing is a spiritual longing. He correctly diagnoses it, and then he feeds it. He recalls a time when he encountered God — "I have seen you in the sanctuary and beheld your power and your glory" (verse 2).

The word "seen" that David uses here (*chazah* in Hebrew) is a word frequently used for visionary prophetic experience. He had a vision somewhere along his spiritual journey, and in this moment of intense spiritual hunger, he chooses to recall this visionary encounter he had with God. Why? Because it feeds his spiritual hunger, it motivates him to seek God, and he wants more of God. Recalling his encounter increases his longing for God. He embraces that hunger; he feeds the fire. He recalls the experience, and it draws him back to the Living Water for another soul-satisfying drink.

David goes on to say he will think of God in the night — he will seek God on a night watch. He longs for God, and he commits to seek God through the watches of the night. He feels the desire, increases the desire, and acts on the desire. He turns desire into Godward intentionality. This is the behavior of a masterful River-dwelling follower of God.

To increase my spiritual desires, I love reading books. There are two types of books in particular that feed my hunger: spiritual classics, and biographies of great spiritual men and women who have gone deep with God.

I have read almost everything that A.B. Simpson, Andrew Murray, George Mueller, and many other old saints have written. I have read many of the books by A.W. Tozer, who often mentions what he calls "the Christian mystics." These were people who believed in and experienced supernatural encounters with a living God. Many of those Tozer points to are ancient writers like Madame Guyon, Brother Lawrence, Teresa of Avila, and St. John of the Cross. Reading people who have a passionate thirst for the presence of God inspires me. They expect and seek a personal relationship with God that is real and interactive. They believe in and pursue God's direct revelation, like Corrie ten Boom did. They expect God to lead them and guide them through life, and He does. These saints who have gone before me stir the longings within me for God Himself.

I also read books on prayer frequently. George Mueller wrote a book called *Answers to Prayer* that I read five times in one year, and I turned around the next year and read it several more times. It moved me and inspired me to pursue God.

I love reading Corrie ten Boom, whom I have mentioned several times. She is one of my all-time favorite saints. Sadly, when I mention her today to an audience, many people do not know her. She and her family helped Jewish people escape from the Nazis in WW2, and they ended up being arrested. Her sister, Betsie, died in the concentration camp, and Corrie suffered much there. God used the platform of her suffering to launch her into a ministry that touched hundreds of thousands of people. Her book, *Tramp for the Lord*, tells of her experience in ministry traveling around the world by faith as an evangelist, and may be one of the clearest examples of what a revived life looks like that I have ever read.

Corrie ten Boom lived a Kingdom lifestyle — she had been filled with and was living in the fullness of the Spirit. As a result, her life was characterized by the marks of the Spirit's fullness - witness, power, and God's guidance (prophecy). She knew it wasn't because she was something special; she refers to herself often as a "little old Dutch woman." She was simply a River Dweller, and the fruitfulness of her life was a direct result of the

Spirit's presence.

I intentionally saturate my life with a steady stream of books which feed my soul and increase my spiritual longing. Just in the past few months, I have read biographies on George Whitefield, John Wesley, Jonathan Edwards, William Carey, D.L. Moody, and George Mueller. The lives of these great saints inspire me to be a man of the Spirit; they increase my hunger for God's presence in my life.

When I spend time with other people who are passionately pursuing the presence of God, their lives call me to the River. I love to spend time with someone who has been dwelling in the River, because being with them increases my desire for God. I love engaging in dialogue with someone who is passionate for God, because his or her fire fuels my fire. Is your life so marked with the Spirit that when people are with you, they long to be with God? If not, isn't that the life you want?

I need long blocks of time alone with God to continue to keep my spiritual hunger growing, to deepen my intimacy with Him, and to increase my awareness of God's presence. I go on spiritual retreats every two months; I've done it for years now. I go to a monastery that is about two hours from my house. Most of the time, I am there for two days. I leave early in the morning on a Tuesday and come home in time for my children's arrival from school on a Wednesday.

The monastery is very quiet and remote. Usually I don't even get a cell phone signal there — which is one of the reasons I love it. I can give my full, undistracted attention to God for an extended period of time. I go there to be alone with God, because I need Him. My heart longs for God, and being there has only increased that longing. Often as I drive up onto the campus, I can feel the Spirit of God refreshing me. It is like taking a deep breath of fresh, clean air. I can feel the breath of the Spirit coming into my soul, renewing me as I set aside extended time to be with Him.

I have discovered cultivating spiritual desire is a critically important component in developing intimacy with God. Longing fuels my pursuit of God; longing intensifies my love for God; and longing helps keep my eyes peeled for the subtle appearances of God's Spirit in my life. I think too many of us are spiritually starved and emaciated because we simply spend too little time cultivating intimacy with God. We are too busy, and our souls suffer from our hurried lives. We run to broken cisterns to quench our spiritual thirst instead of going to the River of Life. As River Dwellers, we must embrace the spiritual longings that are deep within us and welcome them as invitations by the Spirit of God into the River of Life. What are the things that feed your spiritual hunger? Discover and engage in those activities.

Silence

One last thing that has really helped me cultivate my spiritual longing is silence. I mentioned silence as a discipline that has helped me to stay in the River. It has also greatly increased my spiritual appetite for God. David said, "For God alone my soul waits in silence" (Psalm 62:1).

Words can sometimes distract me from being present with another. Have you ever had a conversation with someone who was listening to you only so they could tell you what they were thinking? They were waiting for you to finish so they could have their turn to speak. At the end of a conversation like that, you probably didn't feel heard. The person was with you, but they were not present to you.

I can be physically present to my wife without being totally attentive. I have often been guilty of praying words without having my full attention on God. I have been guilty of singing songs of praise while thinking of something else. Sadly, I confess that I have read a whole chapter of Scripture without really paying attention to what I was reading, because my mind was preoccupied with something else. In each of those situations, I was physically there, but not totally present. I was distracted.

Silence helps me to fix my attention on Jesus. It takes practice, because usually when I first come in silence, my mind is jumping all over the place. My to do list is screaming at me. Problems are present to me. I don't give up; instead I keep turning my loving attention to Jesus, because I long for Him.

In silence I come to Him, not for what He can give me, not for some answer to prayer, not for some solution to a problem, not for some comfort for a heartache, not for some healing for a pain. I come for Him and Him alone. *For God alone my soul waits in silence.* I think it is because I come for God alone that He increases my desire for Him. I fix my eyes on Jesus (Hebrews 12:2). I seek to become fully present with Him. I give Him my full attention. As I come, I am confessing with my silence that He is what I need most of all. I can live without all of these other things that distract me, if I just have Him.

A number of years ago, as I had ramped up the silence in my life, I started experiencing something very different. I could sense God's presence. I can often feel His presence with me, so that wasn't unusual. But as I was spending time in silence, while I could feel God's presence, I could also feel this intense longing for God. It was a growing intensity; the more time I spent in silence, the more my heart ached for God's presence. It was so intense that I was moved to tears.

It felt like a very deep soul longing, an inner tug at the depths of my being. There was an emptiness to it, and I knew it was very clearly and distinctly a longing for God. I had never felt this longing for God so clearly or so strongly. I didn't know why I was experiencing it. Why would I be longing for God when I was with God? Why would I long so intensely for Him when I could actually feel Him with me?

It kept happening, so I went to talk to one of the monks at the monastery about it. The monks and I don't agree about all theological points, but we do agree about the most important thing: our love for Jesus and for people. It saddens me that so many people cannot learn from anyone if they disagree with them. If you can only learn from people you agree with, you won't grow very much. If you only allow yourself to learn from people who are like you, you will always hover right about where you are. You can learn from people without compromising the essential truths of God, if you're humble, so I went to Father Robert, who was the guest master at the monastery.

I asked him, "Have you ever been silent before God and had a sense of God's presence, but at the same time, you were longing for God so intensely that you were moved to tears?" He said, "Oh, yes." I asked, "What is that?" He said, "You are longing for Heaven, so you can see Him face to face."

Some years earlier I had read the story of Moses and was deeply impressed by Moses' journey. While at first Moses hid his face from God, he had learned above all else he needed God's presence to succeed on his impossible mission, so he passionately pursued God's face. He became face-to-face friends with God.

I had been pursuing God's face — not His hands, but His face — for many years. I suddenly realized this longing I felt was homesickness. I was homesick for Heaven so I could be with Jesus. I was homesick for the day when the deep longing of my soul would finally be fulfilled — when His presence would fully be revealed. I was homesick for the One who has become my home and my refuge. This longing was intensifying as my love for the Lover deepened.

I travel quite a bit, and when I am away from home, I get homesick often. The worst time was when I was in Ecuador, and I was as sick as I have ever been. I was lying on a bed in an unfamiliar room, in an unfamiliar culture, with unfamiliar smells, feeling horribly sick from food poisoning, and I was longing for home so badly that it moved me to tears. I just wanted to go home.

As I lay there sick on my dingy hotel bed, my computer was on its screensaver, and pictures of my wife and children kept scrolling through. It only provoked this homesick feeling. I've realized it's a powerful thing to have a home that you long for. It is a deeply moving thing to feel such love for someone that you feel homesick when you are not together. It is a beautiful thing to have a place to call home — a place where you feel loved, and safe, and accepted, and at peace.

Every earthly home we long for is merely a shadow of the heavenly home that awaits us. This world we live in is broken; it doesn't work right. It is marred by sin and injustice, by pain, hurts, and unfulfilled longings. It is only natural we should long for home.

When the Spirit of God lives in us, it is only normal for Him to stir longings within us for Heaven and for the face-to-face intimacy with God for which we were created. The ultimate soul-satisfying intimacy with God for which our hearts eagerly long will only be experienced in Heaven. Until we get there, we will taste of that which is to come, but not yet experience it fully. So we long for home.

The longing isn't a bad thing; it is a sign of hope and of better things to come. The longing makes us sensitive to God's presence — it keeps us eagerly searching for Him wherever life finds us, and it reminds us we are but a stranger passing through this temporary land, and we are on our way home. We have a Father there who awaits our arrival. This longing helps me to detach from the things of this world. It helps me to remember that I belong to another place, and the longing helps me attach to the One who awaits my arrival and to the permanent home He has created for me.

If we continually dull the longing with earthly pleasures, we will never be full-time River Dwellers. We may touch the River sometimes. We may live near the River. We may see the River and admire it from a distance. We may even dip our toes in it occasionally. Without embracing the longing for face-to-face intimacy with the Father, we will not be River Dwellers.

One day I spoke at the seminary, and I told this story about my encounter with Father Robert. My friend Ron Walborn came to me after and said, "I'm worried about you, bud." I asked, "Why?" He said, "You talk about Heaven more than anyone I know." I laughed, "You think I'm suicidal?" He said, "The thought crossed my mind." I told him I just longed to go to Heaven because I wanted to be with Jesus and to see Him face to face. He decided longing was OK. Cultivating the longing for God has increased my nearness to Him. It definitely has made me long for Heaven, too. Heaven will solve all earth's problems and fulfill all God's promises. And it will place me face to face with the Savior who loved me so much that He died for me. What's not to long for?

I don't want to just do my devotions. I want to live in His presence. I don't want to just say my prayers and then go to work. I want to be with God in prayer, and then I want to be with God while I am work. I want to live in the River of God all the time — wherever I go, whatever I do, whomever I am with.

Let's cultivate an awareness of God's presence and feed our spiritual desires. Let's become full-time River Dwellers, living in the fullness of the Spirit.

Reflection Questions

Chapter 3: Living in the River

1.   When you feel that nagging emptiness in your soul, what are some of the things you turn to instead of God? Do you misdiagnose spiritual hunger? How can you begin to recognize your spiritual hunger and turn to God instead of other things?

2.   Have you ever experienced the manifest presence of God? Recall a time when you did. What was it like? How did it affect you?

3.   Do you actively seek to cultivate or practice the presence of God? What helps you to access God's presence? How do you recognize God's presence? What could you do to live more consistently in the cultivated presence of God? Are there any changes that you could make that would benefit you?

4.   How can you become more aware of God's presence as you walk through your daily life?

5.   What spiritual disciplines are you currently using in your life to connect with God? Are they helping you to live consistently in the River? What spiritual disciplines could you add that help to expand your experience with God (for example, meditation, worship, thanksgiving, silence, solitude, listening prayer)?

"Revival is just the life of the Lord Jesus poured into human hearts. Jesus is always victorious. . . And we, on our part, have only to get into a right relationship with Him, and we shall see His power being demonstrated in our hearts and lives and service, and His victorious life will fill us and overflow through us to others. And that is Revival in its essence."

Roy Hession, *The Calvary Road*

"Since we live by the Spirit, let us keep in step with the Spirit."

Galatians 5:25

CHAPTER 4

Climbing Out of the River

A while back I was the guest speaker on a Christian college campus for a few days. I love the passion of youth. I love hanging out with young people. I love having a young staff — the majority of my staff are in their twenties and thirties. I love their eagerness, their energy, their passion, and their idealism.

While I was with the college students on the last night, they were passionately worshiping God. It was energizing and moving, but all week long, the students had been confessing sin to me. I had preached on soul care topics including repentance, and they were coming clean with their secrets. I had talked about living in the light with God and others, and they were bringing their sins into the light.

Much of the sin they confessed was related to sexual immorality, which isn't surprising considering their age group. What surprised me was the significant level of their sinful wanderings — several students confessed that they were sleeping with multiple partners a night.

As I stood up to preach after that passionate time of worship, I felt compelled to give a word I sensed was from the Lord to the student body. Actually, I think it is a word from the Lord to this young generation today.

I said, "Many of you really want to see a new spiritual movement. You want to be part of a revival. I think your generation has the potential to usher in a new move of the Spirit. But there is a hole in your souls that is demanding attention. To fill it, you are either going to be sensual, or you are going to be spiritual. You can't be both. If you opt to fulfill your sensual desires with sexual immorality, and other illicit sensual acts, then the next great move of the Spirit won't come. God is holy. If we opt for sin to fill our souls, then we grieve the Spirit. We must choose God."

We often want God to come to us, and we want God to make us feel good. We want God to fill us, but we want to live life on our terms. It just doesn't work that way. God will love you even if you walk in sin, but you can't walk in sin and dwell in the River. If we walk in the light, we will walk with God; if we walk in the darkness, we will walk alone. His presence will be noticeably absent.

I have tried to cultivate sensitivity to the Spirit's presence. I want to recognize God's presence with me at every turn. I don't want to miss Him when He reveals Himself. When I am in the River, I feel peace. There is an inner stillness and calm. It is the peace of Heaven. When I get out of the River, I often feel a sense of angst in my soul. I have become attuned to this; but I had to learn what it felt like.

If we are going to become full-time River Dwellers, we not only need to become sensitive to the presence of God, but we need to become sensitive to the absence of God. We need to recognize the times we have climbed out of the River so we can return quickly. We need to know what it feels like when we have quenched or grieved the Spirit.

Living in the Light

As full-time River Dwellers, it's important we live in the light. Let's look again at this passage from the apostle John:

> "This is the message we have heard from him and declare to you: God is light; in him there is no darkness at all. If we claim to have fellowship with him and yet walk in the darkness, we lie and do not live out the truth. But if we walk in the light, as he is in the light, we have fellowship with one another, and the blood of Jesus, his Son, purifies us from all sin." (1 John 1:5-7)

Light is a powerful image. Light reveals things for what they are. When we turn on the light in a dark room, it doesn't change what is in a room — it merely reveals what is already there.

John says this is what God is like. He is light. He shines the light of the Spirit in our hearts to reveal darkness to us. He shows us where we are out of alignment with God. He does it because spiritual darkness destroys true relationship.

The level of our soul health determines the health of our relationships. If on a scale of one to ten, your soul health is a five, the healthiest relationship you can have is a five. The only way to move from a five to six is to change. This is why God shines light into our souls. He wants us to have a healthy soul and to live in healthy relationships with Him and others. No one can have a healthy and deep relationship if they choose to live in the darkness.

There are two relationships here John says are affected by our living in the light or in the dark. First, if you live in the darkness, it is destructive to your relationship with God. God knows your sin. You can't trick Him. You can't fool Him. He knows what is there in your soul. John is very direct about this with us: "If we claim to have fellowship with him and yet walk in the darkness, we lie and do not live out the truth" (verse 6). You can lie to yourself. You can lie to others. But you can't lie to God.

If you walk in the dark, it impairs your relationship with God. To be clear: He will still love you. If you choose to walk in the dark, it will damage your relationship with Him, and you will feel distant from Him. His omnipresence will still be with you. God is always present everywhere at all times. But His manifest presence will be withdrawn, and the sense of the cultivated presence we discussed in the last chapter will be greatly diminished. When we choose to walk in the darkness, we climb out of the River of Life. We cannot live in the River and continue to ignore the Spirit's call to repent of sin.

Sin grieves the Holy Spirit. It isn't just our relationship with God that is affected by our sins. Our sins also affect others. In verse 7, John writes, "If we walk in the light, as he is in the light, we have fellowship with one another."

There is a corollary implication here — if we walk in the dark, it will harm our fellowship with one another. We cannot rise above the level of darkness in our souls. It impacts our soul health and all of our relationships.

For example, imagine you had a disagreement with someone. In the disagreement, you used some words and tones that were less than gracious and loving. You were sarcastic and insensitive, and the other person was hurt. You could see they were hurt, but you pressed on through the conversation and left without cleaning up the offense. Even at the time, you could sense the Holy Spirit was offended because you hurt this person for whom Jesus died, but you justified your words and didn't pay much attention to the unsettled feelings in your soul.

Later the person came to you and told you they were hurt by your comments. You could continue to make excuses, and you could explain why you said what you said. You could defend yourself. You could point out how the other person said some things that offended you, too. If you have grieved the Spirit by your unloving words, none of those justifications will get you back in alignment with the Spirit and with the other person. As the person explains the offense, you sense the Spirit's conviction, which is accompanied by an unsettled soul awareness of the withdrawal of God's tangible presence. The only thing that will get you back into right relationship with the Spirit is to admit your sin, to repent, and to ask for forgiveness. As the light shines, we must accept the light as a gift from God that allows us to return to the presence of God with spiritual sensitivity and allows us to walk in fellowship with others, as well. There is no other path back.

Sometimes we are too quick to apologize and too slow to let the light of the Spirit really penetrate our souls. Someone comes to us with an offense, and they say, "When you said this, it hurt me." We say, "I'm sorry. I'm so sorry." They are gracious and say they forgive us, but many times it doesn't stick, because we are offering a cup worth of forgiveness for a five gallon offense. This is why, so often, the offended party will bring up the conversation again later on. We will say, "I thought we already talked about this; I apologized and you forgave me." The offense was not cleared and the relationship was not reconciled, because we offered a cup worth of apology, and they offered a cup worth of forgiveness. There was a five gallon offense that needed to be addressed.

If we are going to walk in the light, we need to be slow to apologize and quick to listen. I don't mean that we should be reluctant to apologize. Rather, we need to allow the weight of our sin to penetrate our hearts and lead us to godly sorrow and sincere apologies that match the weight of our offense. We often apologize quickly to get out from the discomfort of the light, but in doing so, we don't allow the light to do its deep, soul-cleansing work. As a result, we live at a distance from the Spirit, and if we continue to live life this way, we can become desensitized to the Spirit's presence.

Truth is not an intrusion. It is a gift. It would be far better if we would slow down when someone comes to us with an offense and really make sure we feel the weight of our sin. The more we feel the impact our sin has on others, the deeper the light of the Spirit penetrates our souls, and the more likely we are to turn away from our sin. The further we turn from sin, the more deeply into the River we wade. But, if we apologize too quickly to get away from our discomfort, we are likely to return to our sin over and over because we have failed to realize how grievous our behavior is to God and others. I learned this the hard way in my relationship with Jen. I was quick to apologize, but slow to change.

When Jen and I first got married, I was struggling with lust. I had confessed to the Lord, but even though I confessed each time I fell into sin, I still felt far from God. It was almost like I was lost in the woods and couldn't find my way back to the River.

One day I went to my office where I have many books, and I asked the Lord for help. I prayed, "Lord, I'm stuck, and I don't know why. I feel this absence of Your presence, but I'm not sure why or how to fix it. I need You to help me. Lead me to a verse or a book that will help me. I need wisdom from someone who has gone on before me and knows more than I do."

I had an eight-foot bookshelf in my office, and I sensed the Spirit say to me, "You put a book up on that tall shelf because you thought you would never read it. Reach up there and get it. You need it now."

I reached up, patted around, and found the book. It was Norman Grubb's book, *Continuous Revival.* I started reading right away. Grubb talked about this passage in 1 John 1. He emphasized that if we truly walk in the light with God, then we will have fellowship with one another. Grubb said the only reason why we don't walk in the light with one another is because of pride. We are more concerned with looking good than we are with being good. God opposes the proud, and He gives grace to the humble.

If I present to you my best self — my prettied up version of me — and you love me, I will not feel loved. The problem is you aren't loving the real me; you are loving some pretend me I carefully present to you. I can only experience love if I present myself to you as I really am. We can only live in true community if we are honest and gracious with one another. The light of God can tear down the walls of pretension, but we must be willing.

To walk in the light with God and others, and not to be pretentious, requires humility. As Norman Grubb was calling me to walk in the light with God and others, I could sense the Holy Spirit urging me to confess my lust to Jen. I was sitting in bed reading. She was sitting right next to me reading a book of her own. I was feeling terribly uncomfortable. I silently told the Lord, "I could confess lust to another guy — to one of my friends. They would understand. I can't tell Jen. She'll cry. I'll feel bad. She'll feel bad. It's a bad idea all around, God."

The Spirit was relentless. I argued, "You don't understand. You've never been married!" It seemed like a reasonable defense to me at the time. He persisted in convicting me to tell Jen and to come into the light with her.

I did what any man of God would do. I shut off the light and went to bed. But I couldn't sleep. I lay there tossing and turning. Finally, I couldn't take it anymore. I said, "Sweetie, are you awake?" She said, "Who could sleep with you tossing and turning like that?" I fumbled in, "I'm sorry. I need to talk to you." She said, "It's about time." I pushed on through the darkness and told her I was struggling with lust. She cried (I knew it!). I felt the weight of my sin. The power of the light broke the darkness in my soul. Light always dispels darkness. Best of all, it got me back in the River. It strengthened my relationship with Jen, too. It was hard for her, but my hiddenness had put up an invisible wall between us that my openness and repentance was able to dismantle. We were back in the light with God and each other, and true fellowship was restored.

It is only by walking in the light that we can have fellowship with God and with one another. The most important thing in the entire world is to love God and love people. When we get out of the River of Life, God shines light into our souls so that we will return to the River and live in loving relationships. It's a gift. To ignore the gift of light is to do so at our own peril.

I love Charles Dickens' classic, *A Christmas Carol*. It is my all-time favorite novel. Scrooge is a man who has spent most of his life walking in the darkness, and it has shriveled his soul. God offers him a gift of light. He sends his old partner, Jacob Marley, and three other ghostly visitors to show him the truth. When the first ghost appears, the Ghost of Christmas Past, he has light beaming from his head. Scrooge felt terribly uncomfortable in the presence of the light, and he begged the spirit to put on his cap and cover his light-drenched head. "What!" exclaimed the Ghost, "would you so soon put out, with worldly hands, the light I give?" Scrooge has to make a choice. He can embrace the light God offers and accept the truth about himself, as painful as it is, or he can continue to cling to the darkness. What he cannot choose is to remain in the darkness and walk with God. That is never an option, for God is light, and in Him there is no darkness. To reject the light is to reject God Himself. Scrooge finally chooses to accept the gift of light, and he is transformed.

We must make the same choice as Scrooge. We can either embrace the light God offers as a gift, or we can cling to the illusions of the darkness. God won't force us to accept the gift He offers.

Revealing our Sin

The Spirit of God shines light into our souls for three purposes: to reveal our sins, to reveal our secrets, and to increase our self-awareness. First, the Holy Spirit shines light into our life to reveal our sins. God doesn't do this to condemn you. He shines light into your soul about your sin so you will repent.

In the early days after I was baptized with the Spirit, I was learning how to walk in the fullness of the Spirit, and I would feel the peace of God robbed from my heart when I sinned. I didn't know what it was. I went to a social gathering one night, and we were sitting around talking to a bunch of people. I came home, and this inner peace was gone. It felt similar to what I feel if I have too much coffee. I was jittery; my soul was anxious.

At first, I thought I had too much coffee, but long after the caffeine should have worn off, I was still feeling this inner uneasiness. I went to God and asked Him why I was feeling this.

Part of developing sensitivity to God's presence is going to God when things are amiss. Too often we feel something is amiss and we ignore it. We must pay attention to the disruptions of our soul and ask God for wisdom. I went to God that night, and He reminded me of something that I had said at the party that was insensitive to someone's feelings. I called the person and asked for forgiveness, and immediately the peace of God returned. I was beginning to learn what it felt like to walk in the fullness of the Spirit, to dwell in the River.

1 John 1:9 says, "If we confess our sins, he is faithful and just and will forgive us our sins and purify us from all unrighteousness." God shines the light to show us sin so He can purify us. His desire is that we can turn from sin so we can gain victory over it, and our relationships will be healthy with Him and with others. Sin separates us from God's intimate presence. Repentance returns us to the River. We must develop sensitivity to the Spirit's grief over our sin if we are going to become full-time River Dwellers.

When the Spirit reveals our sin, our responsibility is to stand in the light with it. Accept the gift of light that He offers. His light is our call back to the River of Life. Heed the call. When God shows us a sin in our life, our immediate response needs to be, "Yes, God, that is true about me."

Imagine you go to a friend's house one night for dinner. This is a fairly new friend, and it is the first time that you are going to their house. You have really enjoyed getting to know this person, and you are looking forward to an evening together. The dinner is wonderful, the company is engaging, and you have a marvelous time. Your friend's house is absolutely gorgeous — in fact, if you were to design your dream house, many of the features in this house would be in the home you designed. As they take you on a tour, you ooh and aah.

You finish your evening together, and as you pull into your driveway, you begin to notice all the things that are wrong with your house. The roof is getting old and will soon need to be replaced. Some of the trim needs painting. One of the shutters is cockeyed, and the inside of the house needs even more work. It seems old and drab and in desperate need of updates. Even if you finished all the work to perfection, the house is still lacking — it just isn't designed properly.

You started the evening with anticipation. You had a marvelous time of fellowship. Now you are grumpy and irritated. As you find yourself beginning to grumble and complain, you sense the Spirit of God convicting you. Something is amiss inside your soul. There is that old, familiar, unsettled feeling within you. Somewhere underneath all your muttering is a still, small voice trying to get your attention. The word He is whispering to you is "envy." You have crossed the line into covetousness, and the Spirit is shining light into your soul to draw you back into the River.

At that moment, your only proper response is to let the light do its work and simply say, "Yes, God, that's true about me. I am struggling with covetousness. I envy my friend's house. Forgive me. Thank you for what you have given me. I have a good home, and I have an eternal dwelling place that is far more important. Thank you for what you have given my new friends, and for the new friendship. Thank you for what you have given to them, and that they shared it with me." As you pray this prayer of confession and thanksgiving, you make your way back to the River where everything lives. There is no life in sin; there is only death there.

The most obvious hindrance to our River Dwelling is sin. In Ephesians 4:30, Paul writes, "Do not grieve the Holy Spirit." Sin grieves the Spirit. Paul told the church in Galatia, "So I say, walk by the Spirit, and you will not gratify the desires of the sinful nature" (Galatians 5:16). Our sinful nature is just our natural propensity to go our own way, to walk away from God, and to get out of the River.

Our sinful nature and the Spirit are in conflict. The sinful nature is calling us out of the River and calling us to the self-life. The sinful nature calls us to rely on our self to fulfill our inner longings. There is an inner emptiness inside, and the sinful nature demands it to be filled. It tells us we have a right to be filled. It constantly demands, "What about me? What's in it for me?"

The sinful nature is never grateful, never satisfied. It always demands to be attended to and has a plethora of excuses and justifications for all of its sinful demands. The direction of the sinful nature, though, is always out of and away from the River of Life. The enemy of our souls feeds into our sinful nature. He calls us away from God and into the woods, promising that our soul hunger will be satisfied there through his illicit bounty. He speaks soothingly to our sinful nature to assure us that our desires for comfort and convenience are perfectly justifiable, noble even. Paul says if we are going to overcome this internal struggle, we are going to have to walk by the Spirit.

The Holy Spirit shines light into our souls so we will acknowledge our sin and get back into right alignment with Him, but He does not expect us to change on our own. Life change is a byproduct of living in right relationship with God. As we are in the River, God gives us the power to overcome these difficult sin patterns in our life. The enemy will sometimes point out our sin, too. He does it to condemn us and then to hang our sin over us in shame and try to get us to change in our own strength. This isn't so with God. He wants us to turn from our sin, and turn to Him. Walking with the Spirit gives us the power to overcome sin. It isn't by more human effort that we discover victory; it is by living in the River that we become more Christ-like.

Paul continues, "Since we live by the Spirit, let us keep in step with the Spirit" (Galatians 5:25). Paul uses this image of walking with God. He is the guide, and we are walking alongside of Him. He knows His way. He knows what is best, and He longs for our best. We are chatting and doing life together — keeping step together — and we're in fellowship with God. Then all of a sudden the Guide tells us to turn right. It may be to turn away from an improper relationship that is forming. It may be to turn away from greed or covetousness or anger that is quickly turning to bitterness. We don't want to go right; we don't want to turn away. We see something off in the woods that interests us. The tempter is promising us if we go after this thing in the woods it will satisfy, so we leave the path. We leave the Guide, and we wander off into the woods. We are out of step with the Spirit.

We were in proper alignment with God, and then we turned aside; we went our own way and got out of alignment. As a result, God shines light into our souls to show us that we have sinned. He is calling us back to the path, back into a rightly aligned relationship with Him. We must repent quickly, and get back in step with the Spirit. If we don't keep our confessions current, we will find ourselves deep into the woods, and we'll lose sight of the River. We will grieve the Spirit.

Too often we tolerate sin but become unwittingly intolerant to the River Dwelling life. If we refuse the light God offers, and we continue to go our own way, God will still love us. But our relationship will be damaged, and our soul will move toward increasing levels of unhealthiness. Sin is never without consequences, and this is why the God who loves us calls us to repent. If we are going to get in the River and stay in the River, we must follow the Spirit — we need to keep in step with our Guide.

While Paul uses the image of walking with the Spirit, John uses the image of the River. They are talking about the same concept with a different analogy. Think of the image John uses about the River. The Holy Spirit is like a River within us. He is the River of Life. Everything that gets in the River lives. There is abundant life in the River.

So here we are, in the River with God. We are experiencing the fullness of God. We can feel joy and peace and love. We are hearing the promptings of the Spirit, and the fruit of the Spirit is coming forth in our lives. One day we see something on the shores that intrigues us. It allures us; it appeals to our sinful nature, our self-life. Satan, our adversary, calls us over to check it out. He lies and tells us this thing will satisfy that longing in our souls. We paddle over to the shore as we tell ourselves, "I'm just going to take a peek."

When we get there, we like what we see, and we decide to check it out some more. Listen: The whole way over to the shore, the Spirit of God is shining light in our heart. He is whispering to us and telling us, "Don't do it. Don't go there. It isn't worth the trip. Come to me. Stay in the River. Only I can satisfy."

We ignore the Spirit's promptings and convictions, and we get out of the River. Still, the Spirit beckons us back. He convicts us. He calls us. He tells us to leave sin behind.

We can ignore God. We can refuse His light, and He will still love us. There is a price to our disobedience, though: It will damage our relationship with God, and it will rob our souls from the fullness of life in the River. Sadly, ignoring the conviction of the Spirit often results in our becoming dull to His voice. If we continue to get further away from the River, further into the woods, then His voice becomes faint. Our hearts become hard, and conviction no longer gets through to our deadened hearts.

God actually leaves us to our choice. We fall under what Paul describes as the Law of Harvest. In Galatians 6:7-8, he writes, "Do not be deceived: God cannot be mocked. People reap what they sow. Those who sow to please their sinful nature, from that nature will reap destruction."

In other words, darkness destroys. It leaves us distant from God and others, and it leaves our soul in ruins. This is not what God wants for your life or mine. He wants us to have life and life abundant. He wants us to live in the River. The consequence of refusing His invitation to live in the River is destruction.

We must learn to tune into the conviction of the Holy Spirit, and we must learn to respond quickly. We cannot ignore His voice and continue to make our way further into the River. Today, if you are out of the River, turn back. Perhaps you have been stuck in a sin pattern for quite some time. You feel like you are walking with God, and then you fall down and find yourself in the gutter. You get up, only to fall down again over the same sin pattern. You confess, and get back on the road, but after a few steps you fall down again. You are disheartened. I have been there, too. Keep getting up. Keep turning your eyes to Jesus. Keep living in the light with God and others. The only way you are truly defeated by sin is if you decide to quit fighting and lay down in the gutter or if you decide to take consolation in the darkness rather than walk in the light. If you decide to camp out in the woods, you will never be a River Dweller. You may end up living along the edge of the River for a while, dipping in and out of the River. You have to keep returning to the Living Water. When you sin, confess. When you fall, get up. When you get out of the River, get back in.

Revealing our Secrets

The Holy Spirit also shines light into our lives to reveal our secrets. Secrets may be one of the single most destructive forces to the soul on the planet. In Psalm 32, David says:

> *"Blessed are those whose transgressions are forgiven, whose sins are covered. Blessed are those whose sin the Lord does not count against them and in whose spirit is no deceit. When I kept silent, my bones wasted away through my groaning all day long. For day and night your hand was heavy on me; my strength was sapped as in the heat of summer. Then I acknowledged my sin to you and did not cover up my iniquity. I said, 'I will confess my transgressions to the Lord.' And you forgave the guilt of my sin."* (Psalm 32:1-5)

David was hiding. He had secret sin. He didn't confess it to God or others, and it was killing him. It was such a destructive force upon his soul that it began to have physical effects on him. He says his bones were wasting away. Sometimes we have confessed these sins to God, but no one else knows. This kind of secrecy often still blocks us from God's fullness — that was my experience in the story I told earlier about struggling with lust. Secrets become barriers to God's presence.

I have prayed for people who came to me with a physical problem and asked me to pray for healing. When I prayed, I took time to listen to the Spirit, and I sensed the Lord prompting me to ask them if they had any unconfessed sin. I have seen cases where as soon as the person confessed their secrets, their physical problems were healed without anyone even praying for healing. This is why James instructs us to confess our sins to one another when we are praying for the sick.

James 5:14-16, "Is anyone among you sick? Let them call the elders of the church to pray over them and anoint them with oil in the name of the Lord. And the prayer offered in faith will make them well; the Lord will raise them up. If they have sinned, they will be forgiven. Therefore confess your sins to each other and pray for each other so that you may be healed." Not all sickness is caused by sin. But there are times when a physical problem arises because of sin, and there are times when the block to physical healing is a secret sin.

I have met with people who were being plagued by emotional troubles — like panic attacks or depression. When I prayed for them about the emotional problems, once again, the Lord revealed that they had a secret. Only after the secret was exposed did the panic attacks stop or the depression lift. Of course, not all emotional troubles are due to sin, but David was experiencing some oppression because of his hiddenness.

I have listened to so many stories of people who have been crushed under the weight of family secrets like affairs, molestation, addiction, and violence. I have seen and heard the terrible, destructive nature of family secrets. We must bring the secrets to the light, or we won't have fellowship with God and others. We can't bring healing to our souls or to our families as long as we are going to harbor our secrets.

Secrets are destructive to the soul, and their damage can leak into our physical and emotional health. When it comes to the inner life, bad things grow in the dark. We must live in the light with God and others.

I teach a course called Soul Care. I designed the course because I learned some key principles on my own journey toward wholeness that I wished someone would have taught me while I was still in seminary. As I have taught Soul Care over the years, many times I have had people come up to me and say these now famous words: "I've never told anyone this before." They then proceed to confess some shameful sin, and it is painful to watch.

Steeped in shame, they look down at the floor, shuffle back and forth, and stammer over their words. It is incredibly hard to come clean with a secret, but it is so rewarding. Often after the confession, and the prayer and the tears and the Lord's presence and grace, I can look at the person and see the weight of the world has been lifted from them.

Bringing secrets to the light also restores relationships. I can't tell you how many times a person went home after confessing to me and told their spouse this dark secret they had been carrying around. As painful as it was for them to tell the truth and for their partner to hear the truth, in the end, there was healing not only for the confessor but also for the relationship.

I have talked to many spouses over the years who said to me, "I knew there was a block in our relationship. I could feel it, but I didn't know what it was. After they told me, and we walked through forgiveness, and reestablished trust, our relationship has gone to a whole new place. The block is gone."

Darkness destroys relationships, but light is a powerful thing. There is no life in the woods, but everything that gets into the River lives! There is no way to live in the River and to live in secrecy. We must live in the River at all costs. I guarantee that it will cost you and me our pride if we are going to be full-time River Dwellers. Our pride longs to be secretive and to present ourselves better than we really are, but we cannot walk in pride and live in the River. We must humble ourselves.

I was speaking at a seminar a few years ago. A man brought his wife to me one day hoping I would be able to "fix" her. She was cold and angry, and she obviously did not want to be there or to talk to me. I have learned to respect people's freedom. I said to her, "I can see you aren't here by your own volition. If you get to the place where you want help, let me know."

I could also sense that she had secrets. I very gently told her if she were going to get help, she would have to come into the light with her secrets. A few months later, she reached out to me. She was ready. She confessed all her hidden sin. She forgave her husband, who had hurt her deeply. Underneath her secrets and bitterness were some demonic strongholds that we prayed through. And that day, God met this woman in a powerful prayer time.

I saw her several months later when I was back in the area. She came running up to me to give me a hug, but I didn't recognize her. Her countenance had changed so much I didn't realize who she was. Her hard, angry, defiant demeanor had been replaced with joy, light, and freedom. As she hugged me and thanked me for how much that day had changed her life, I was shocked to realize this was the same woman. I have seen her many times since that day of her deliverance, and she continues to dwell in the River, free and full. It is a powerful thing to walk in the light.

A note to those of you who are reading this and are feeling a tug to step into the light: If you are going to come clean with others, you might want to get some help to do it wisely. When you reveal secrets, it is incredibly painful to you and to others, and it might require some wise guidance to see you through to the other side where healing waits. It's worth it, but I encourage you to get help.

Life is better when we walk in step with God. It is the call of the Spirit to get out of the woods and into the River. If you are in the woods today, hiding in secret, heed the call, humble yourself, and get back to the River. The Spirit grieves for you until you return.

Increasing Our Self-Awareness

The Holy Spirit also shines light into our lives to increase our self-awareness. We will never rise above our level of self-awareness. If you are in the dark about something in your life, you cannot walk in victory over it.

For example, if you are completely unaware that you are a fearful person, or unaware of how your fear influences you, then you will try to control and manipulate others out of fear. You will not walk in victory over those controlling behaviors until you admit the fear and the controlling behavior. Even when people approach you about it, and confront you, you will make excuses. You will explain and justify your behavior, and you will try to convince people this is just the way you are. You will not walk free from the fearful and controlling behavior until you admit you have it.

This is why the first step for an alcoholic is to admit that they are an alcoholic. The person who says, "I'm not an alcoholic; sometimes I just drink too much," is not on their way to freedom. They are still in denial, and we can never rise above our level of self-awareness.

People who lie to themselves walk in bondage, sadly unaware. I've always loved this quote by Francis Bacon: "It is a sad fate for a man to die too well known to everybody else and still unknown to himself." Often others can see the truth that we deny about ourselves. The Spirit of God will bring you opportunities to see the truth about yourself. He will shine the light into your soul, and sometimes the light will come through another person. You must accept the light that God offers. If you deny it, and excuse it, and justify it, you will continue to do the very things that are destructive to your relationships. Sadly, the result will be that you will find yourself in painful relationships and far from the presence of God. The Spirit of God is a gentleman. He will not force truth upon us. He offers it gently as a gift, and we must receive it humbly. Refusing the gentle gift of light results in a sense of the absence of God, because God is light. God shines truth into our lives. To reject the truth is to reject God Himself. We are refusing the approach of His presence.

In my own life I had a problem with insecurity that particularly affected my relationship with Jen; I would feel threatened when Jen disagreed with me. Feeling insecure isn't a sin. But being unaware of insecurity can lead to sinful behavior and broken relationships. When Jen disagreed, I would vigorously express my ideas and defend myself to her, trying to vindicate myself and convince her of my way of thinking. Jen felt stomped on by the power of my opinions. I noticed I would get more intense in these conversations. I noticed my heart rate would increase, and my RPM's would speed up. I was aware that Jen would withdraw. After one of these conversations, I would sense this restlessness and notice the peace of God was missing. I knew something wasn't right. I just assumed it was because conflict was uncomfortable. I had no idea why I was doing what I was doing, and my lack of self-awareness was destructive. Darkness always is.

The Spirit of God was trying to make me aware of this area of my life and how it was affecting my soul and my relationships with Him and others, most notably Jen. I was refusing the light. At first it was subtle. I could feel that gnawing, uneasy feeling of not being in right alignment with God. I could see from Jen's body language something wasn't right; she was offended. It didn't alter my course. I was too often more interested in being right than I was in being in right relationship. Those close to me were being hurt, and God was trying to get my attention.

Finally, Jen grew so distant from me that the pain of remaining distant became greater than the pain of change. I realized I was part of the problem. I stopped making excuses for my behavior. For years I would tell myself, "This is just the way I am. I'm a passionate person, and I'm just expressing my opinions." If you are going to travel with God in the light, you need to send all of your excuses packing. God is truly a gentleman. He will not force people to receive the light and to change. When we get to a place where we are open to change, He will give the light we need.

I had no idea fear was motivating my powerful opinions and leading me to stomp on others. When I was open to learn, God showed the roots of my behaviors. He led me on a journey of self-discovery. He revealed to me I had a fear of not being loved, and this fear was at the root of my anxiety over conflict and my need to win. Until I became aware of it, I had no chance to overcome it and to change the behaviors associated with it. I was doomed to continue hurting people around me. As I hurt the people around me, I was climbing out of the River.

Just becoming aware of something doesn't give you victory over it. Self-awareness gives you a chance to start to overcome. It opens a doorway in your life for healing and change. We can't change until we stand in the light. As God reveals new truths about yourself, He will lead you to tools of transformation. He will guide us and empower us to victory if we stay in step with Him.

Our lack of self-awareness becomes a lid in our lives, a gateway to darkness. Once I welcomed the light of God, and He brought me new self-discovery, I could fight against the destructive patterns in my life. I gave Jen permission to call me on it, so I could overcome it. I wish I could tell you I am now completely better and I never offend anyone with my strong opinions. I still stomp on Jen's opinions (and others). However, I do it less often, I am more aware of it, and now when I take that path, it cuts me to the heart. If we completely refuse the light that God offers, and deny the truth about ourselves, we will never overcome. We can never rise above our level of self-awareness.

We aren't going to be perfect. It takes one day longer than a lifetime to be perfect; when we meet Him face to face, we shall be like Him. In the meantime, we are on a journey. We don't have to be perfect to live in God's presence consistently, but we do need to live in the light with God and others.

Our sins, our secrets, and our lack of self-awareness often lead us to grieve the Spirit. If we are going to live in the continual fullness of the Spirit, then we must become sensitive to the grieving of the Spirit in our lives. We will never live in freedom beyond the level of light that we walk in.

Quenching the Spirit

Grieving the Spirit is one way we climb out of the River, and quenching the Spirit is another. Paul uses this phrase "quenching the Spirit" in 1 Thessalonians 5:19-20, when he says, "Do not put out the Spirit's fire. Do not treat prophecies with contempt." Some translations, like the ESV and NRSV, say, "Do not quench the Spirit."

This passage is connected to listening to the promptings of the Spirit. If the Spirit is speaking to us, and we are ignoring His promptings, it puts out His fire. It quenches the Spirit. Part of the mark of the Spirit's presence and fullness, as we looked at earlier, is that we hear His voice. But if we hear it, and don't obey it, we quench the Spirit; we get out of the River. Listening to the voice of God is critical to accessing His presence, and ignoring the voice of God inevitably leads to distance in our relationship.

Think about this on a human level. We have all had a time where we were talking to someone, and they weren't listening. They were reading something, or watching TV, or playing on their phone. They made the appropriate "hmm," "uh-huh," "yes" and head nods. They really weren't listening to us at all. Later we reminded them of something from the conversation, and they said, "You never told me that!" It is frustrating when it happens to us, but, of course, we've done the same thing to others and even to God. If it happens a lot, it can be really hurtful to the relationship. We feel unvalued, unnoticed, and even unloved.

The Spirit of God wants to be listened to when He speaks. It is a matter of honor. He wants us to be sensitive to His voice, so that we can recognize with increased regularity when He is speaking. He wants us to obey Him when He does speak. Sensitivity and obedience are honoring to the Spirit of God.

Sometimes we don't listen to the Spirit of God because He gives us a prompting that is risky, and we aren't willing to take the risk. There have been times where I sensed God telling me to talk to a waitress, or pray for a stranger, and I have been reluctant. It was simply fear. We can act on fear or we can act on faith, but we cannot act on both. If we are going to listen to the Spirit, we are going to have to take risks that make us uncomfortable. The Spirit of God seems a lot less concerned about our comfort than we are. In a society like ours in the United States, we overvalue comfort and undervalue character.

Fear can lead us out of the River. This is why David prayed, "Search me, God, and know my heart; test me and know my anxious thoughts. See if there is any offensive way in me, and lead me in the way everlasting" (Psalm 139:23). We know that sin gets us out of sorts with God, but David asks God to see if there are any anxious thoughts in him, because he realizes fear can get him out of the River. Fear is a powerful motivator that often leads us to disobey God's leadings in our life.

Years ago I had a friend who I had been telling about Jesus. We had grown close, and I thoroughly enjoyed our friendship. I had shared the gospel with him, and he had dialogued with me respectfully, but I wasn't sure he really understood the gospel message of Jesus and its ramification for his life. The Spirit of God was pressing me to make the gospel and its implications clear to him. I confess I was nervous to have the conversation, because I valued the friendship, and I wasn't sure how he would respond. The Spirit continued to prompt me to tell him the Good News with boldness, so one day I took him out to lunch.

I said, "I want to explain to you what I believe. I know we have talked about it, but I don't think you understand." He said, "I understand." I pressed on, "I believe that Jesus was the Son of God." He said, "I believe that." I said, "I believe he died for our sins on the cross and he rose again and is currently at the right hand of God the Father." He nodded and said, "I believe that." I said, "I believe Jesus is the only path to forgiveness and a right relationship with God, and all those outside of faith in Christ are separated from God." He said, "I don't believe that."

I went on to explain why I believed that from the Scriptures, and I pleaded with him to understand the gospel. I said to him, "I love you like a brother, and I would never be able to live with myself if I didn't make this crystal clear to you and give you every opportunity to repent and follow Christ." We had a very loving and clear conversation, but he didn't trust Christ at that time. Many years later, though, he moved from our area and ended up following Jesus. That conversation we had over lunch was a seed planted in his soul that eventually came to harvest. We need to risk more than we are comfortable with in order to follow the promptings of the Spirit.

Sometimes we quench the Spirit because we aren't developing ears to hear. We may be too busy. Everyone is busy, but Jesus was busy, too. The difference is Jesus managed to live a busy life with an unhurried soul. He never let His outward activity interfere with His inner quiet. He had a still center that allowed Him to hear God's still, small voice. He didn't allow the demands of people's needs to rob Him of His alone time with the Father. He would get up while it was still dark to meet alone with the Father. And it was these moments alone with the Father, in the still of the morning, that allowed Him to carry a quietness in His soul, even in the busyness of life.

We can't create inner quietness without outer quietness. If we take time in solitude and silence, we can carry our inner quietness into our outer world. If we don't cultivate that inner quiet by being alone with God, then we never put ourselves in a position to be available to the Spirit. It is hard to develop sensitivity to His still, small voice if we are constantly living in inner noise. We have to intentionally develop sensitivity to His voice.

Dashboards of the Soul

In my effort to live more consistently in the River, I have found it helpful to take special notice of the warning signs that indicate I am starting to climb out onto the banks. Think about the dashboard of your car. There are indicator lights on your dashboard that are warning signs. If your oil light comes on, it would be unwise to ignore it. I have heard too many stories of drivers who ignored the oil light only to find they were out of oil and ruined their engine. These indicator lights are there to cause us to pause and to give the car necessary maintenance.

We all have a dashboard of the soul, and there are indicator lights that blink at us and warn us that we are getting out of the River. I'll illustrate the point by giving you my gauges on the dashboard of my soul, but I would encourage you to do some parallel learning and discover your own.

The first gauge that I need to pay attention to on the dashboard of my soul is my compassion gauge. When I am properly connected to the Spirit, His compassion flows in my soul. I can sit and listen to someone's story, and I will be moved with compassion. I often discover what I call "the gift of tears." It is the supernatural compassion of God flowing into my heart.

When I find people are irritating to me, and my compassion is drying up, then I know there is an indicator light blinking at me. My compassion gauge is telling me that something is amiss in my soul. Jesus' compassion has not run dry; I am not in the place where His compassion can flow continuously over my heart. I immediately schedule time alone with God and ask Him what is wrong. I take time to see if I have offended Him or have neglected Him or if my heart has become hardened. I get back into the River as quickly as I can; when I return to the River, the compassion returns to me. The key to living in the River consistently is to recognize when I am getting out of the River and address it immediately. We cannot ignore these warning signs of the soul and continue to dwell in the presence of God.

The second gauge I need to watch is my brokenness gauge. God is irresistibly attracted to the contrite of heart. The passage we looked at earlier in Isaiah 57:15 says that God dwells with the contrite and lowly. His presence is unusually accessible to the contrite. When I am walking in step with the Spirit, sin bothers me. I am quick to admit my sin. When someone comes to me because I have said something that hurt them, and I am broken and contrite, I feel the sting of my sin, and I am moved to tears, often in an apology.

When I am out of the River, I am quite often defensive, and sadly unbroken over my sin. After such an encounter, I know I am in trouble, and I schedule time to get alone with God and to address the condition of my heart so I can get back into the River.

The third gauge I am attentive to is my peace gauge. Colossians 3:15 says, "Let the peace of Christ rule in your hearts." When I am in the River, Christ's peace flows to my soul.

When I feel anxious, I get alone with God to discover the roots of my angst. Anxiety has become one of my key indicator lights. I can't afford to ignore it. It is a sure sign the River water is dripping off my soul. Sometimes I am anxious because I have grieved the Spirit, and I am sensing His conviction. Sometimes I am anxious because I am not walking in restful trust, and I need to get alone with God to surrender the issues that are weighing down my soul. Other times I am anxious because of my overly busy schedule, and my soul is panting in need of rest. I must embrace divine inactivity if I am going to get back in the River and recover the peace of God in my soul. I can't keep up a relentless pace without seasons of rest.

One year I went through an extreme season of busyness. I had just finished a ten-day stint at the seminary teaching Soul Care to doctoral students, on top of all my other responsibilities. I had scheduled some time at the monastery on the heels of this season. As I drove up the long drive on the monastery campus, I started feeling anxious. The angst was strong. I went immediately to my room and began to talk to God about it. I had cultivated the presence of God and with it the peace of God in my life for a long time, and I didn't want to live without it.

I asked the Lord, "Did I sin?" I sensed the Spirit saying, "No." "Am I too busy?" I had a sense that my busyness was not the root of the issue. "Do you want to tell me what this is?" I heard nothing. I was there for three days. All three days I was anxious. I did everything I could to regain my sense of peace. I worshiped. I sat in silence. I listened to the Spirit. But the anxiety continued.

The last day of my stay, I got up and said, "Lord, I can't leave until You tell me how to get rid of this anxiety. I can't live with this." I sensed the Lord calling me to go into the chapel and sit in silence. I sat there for 45 minutes in silence, and finally I heard the whisper of the Spirit: "Psalm 23."

I know Psalm 23, of course; it is probably the most beloved Psalm. "The Lord is my shepherd, I shall not want. He makes me lie down in green pastures, he leads me beside quiet waters, he restores my soul." That was as far as I got. The breath of God blew upon the phrase, "He restores my soul." I lingered with it because I knew God was there in that phrase for me that day.

About 20 minutes later, I heard the Spirit whisper again, "My presence is revealed in many ways. There is my healing presence. My empowering presence. My loving presence. But you need my restorative presence. Your soul has taken on much damage because you have been on the frontlines of battle. You have taken hits, and now you need my restorative presence. It can only be accessed through silence and stillness."

For the next three months, every day I spent multiple times in silence before the Lord. The entire time the anxiety waned, and at the end of the three months it was gone. If we are going to be full-time River Dwellers, we must become sensitive to what is happening in our souls, and to the indicator lights that blink to tell us we are climbing out of the River. If we attend to the required maintenance of the Spirit, we can live consistent lives in His presence.

The fourth gauge I monitor is my passion gauge. Jesus told the church at Ephesus that though they were a good church they had lost their first love (Revelation 2). When I am getting out of the River, there are competitors for my heart's affections. When I am dwelling securely in the River of Life, Jesus is my first love, and I am freshly enamored with His gracious character. If I am no longer moved by the wonder of Jesus, then I need to get alone with Him to check on the condition of my heart and my proximity to the River.

My passion gauge starts to light up for me when I have too many attachments to earthly things. I become attached to these false lovers, and I become overly concerned with things that have far too little eternal value. Often I need to go on a fast to detach from the things of this world, and to reignite my first love for Jesus. When I sense my love running cold or lukewarm, I get alone with God and seek to address it. It is a call from the dashboard of the soul that I cannot afford to ignore.

The fifth gauge I have to keep an eye on is my listening gauge. Jesus said, "My sheep hear my voice" (John 10:27, ESV). When I am in the River, prophecy flows, God's guidance is clear, His loving whispers are with me.

And as I hear and obey the promptings of the Spirit, I sense His life pouring out over my soul. I am refreshed. When I get out of the River, the voice of God becomes faint and distant, and my soul becomes dry and dusty. So if it has been a while since I have heard God's voice, then I need to schedule some soul maintenance and let the Great Physician tinker with my heart. Often I am no longer hearing God clearly because something is amiss in my heart.

The sixth gauge I have to monitor is the stress gauge. My response to stress can pull me out of the River. In times of hardship, difficulties, uncertainties, and turbulence, we may find ourselves tempted to get out of step with the Spirit.

I am a type-A personality. God has gifted me to lead, and I can often make things happen. When things get difficult, and there is a lot of pressure mounting, I internalize that pressure and feel like I have to make something happen as the leader. This internal pressure often causes me to lead out of the flesh, rather than out of the Spirit.

I have had to recognize what it feels like when I am about to lead out of the flesh, because it is one of those places where I find myself on the riverbanks. In times of great pressure, I feel frenetic energy; I feel squirrelly inside. I feel an internal stress and pressure that mounts up within me — there is an increase in adrenalin that makes me want to move at high speed. In these moments, I am tempted to produce spiritual results with a flurry of human activity. I am tempted to push for something rather than trust God for something. Rather than letting the River carry me, I try to lug the River water around on my own.

I don't just push myself. Unfortunately, those around me feel the push, as well. When I act out of this place of stress, fear, pressure, and even anger over the lack of results I am seeing, I can make things happen, because God has given me gifts. When I am leading from that internal chaos, it results in external chaos. We get results, but people get hurt or stressed or weary. I know this is one of those treacherous places for me, and I have to force myself to slow down.

When I feel this internal pressure mounting, I have to get alone with God before I act, lest I act in haste and in the flesh. I need to be still and know He is God (Psalm 46:10). Oftentimes I need a couple of hours alone with God to calm down the inner chaos I feel. I take time to worship and to surrender. I meditate on Scripture, and I sit alone with God in silence. I have to get my eyes off of my circumstances, and put my eyes on Jesus.

Jesus is sitting on His throne today, and He is in perfect peace. He isn't nervous or wringing His hands about my life, saying, "Oh, no! What am I going to do with Rob?" He isn't surprised by my circumstances, nor do they alarm Him. He is in perfect peace, and if I can get my eyes off of me, and off of my circumstances, and onto Him, then He can give me His perfect peace.

We will never feel inner chaos when we are in the River. When we start to feel chaos, and we act on it, we are leaving the River behind. So, when I start to feel this inner chaos, a buildup of internal pressure, I know I need to get alone with God, because the stress gauge on my soul's dashboard is blinking at me. If I take time to slow down and stay in step with the Spirit, then the peace of Heaven overflows into my soul. The circumstances surrounding our life may still be chaotic, but the presence of Jesus brings peace to our inner worlds. It is the peace of Christ that passes all human understanding that trumps all human tragedy (Philippians 4:7).

I have found, in this quiet place with God, I can have a still center even in the midst of turbulent circumstances. Out of that still place from deep within me, where the Spirit of God abides, I can lead from the Spirit — results still come, but this time they produce peace, not chaos. The results produced will come from the Spirit of God, from abiding with Jesus, and not from human effort. This is the kind of River Dwelling life I long to live continually. I have not perfected it. I am not the man I want to be, but I am not the man I used to be either, and I thank God for the progress.

About a year ago, we were facing a very difficult situation in our church. There was a lot of financial pressure and a significant amount of fear. People were acting on fear. There was some negativity, and it was affecting the staff. I had been away on a study break for six weeks, and I came back into this chaos.

The first day back, I felt all this fear building inside of me, and I felt that old familiar pressure to make something happen. As I acted on it, I was contributing to the chaos. I got alone with God for a day. I fixed my eyes firmly on Jesus, and in that time alone with God, I got into the River. I came back and led the staff through the chaos from a very still place in my inner life. Because I was in the River, I was able to carry the presence of God to this chaotic situation. The whole team noticed the difference as we navigated through those difficult times with a sense of God's presence and peace.

Cultivating inner stillness in the midst of chaos can be difficult. But if we intentionally fix our eyes on Jesus and find quiet time alone with Him, He will draw us back to the River, where peace always flows.

What are the gauges in your life that you need to pay attention to? What indicator lights are flashing for you when you are getting out of the River? Are you giving those lights their just due? When they flash, do you call a time out, and get alone with God? These are necessary times for a pit stop.

Paying attention to the dashboard of your soul can greatly increase your River Dwelling capacity.

Guarding Our Hearts

When the dashboard lights start to flash at me, it is most often an indication my heart is in need of attention. To develop sensitivity to the presence or the absence of the Spirit, we must guard our hearts. We must pay attention to the inner life. Proverbs 4:23 says, "Above all else, guard your heart, for it is the wellspring of life" (NIV, 1984).

To guard our heart is to guard it from becoming hard. The soft, humble, contrite heart is essential for River Dwelling. In Isaiah 57:15 the Lord says, "I live in a high and holy place, but also with those who are contrite and lowly in spirit, to revive the spirit of the lowly and to revive the heart of the contrite." These are the two places where God makes His home: in Heaven, and in the heart of the humble, lowly, and contrite.

Humility welcomes the presence of God; pride pushes Him out of the center of our lives. Pride is a River Dweller's greatest enemy, because it hardens our hearts, and a hard heart is not a conducive atmosphere for the presence of God to flow freely. If we present a lowly and contrite heart for God to dwell, He promises He will revive our hearts. He pours out the Living Water over the humble heart that welcomes Him.

Our heart becomes hard sometimes because we don't respond properly when we get hurt. When we are hurt, we take up a shield of self-protection — a shield of anger, or defensiveness, or withdrawal. We do this to protect our hearts from the person who is causing us pain. The problem with a shield is it is indiscriminate — not only does it block out the person who is hurting us, but it also blocks out the presence of God from helping us or healing us. Our hearts grow hard underneath our shields. If we are going to guard our hearts from becoming hard, we must let down our self-protective shields. Only when we let down our shield of self-protection can our heart become soft and sensitive to the presence of God.

For example, if you get hurt in your relationship with your spouse or someone you love deeply, you will often pick up a shield of anger to protect your heart. Some people withdraw when they are angry, and other people attack. The response of anger, withdrawal, or verbal attack becomes the shield that we pick up to protect ourselves. We are hurt, and if we don't pick up these shields, we feel incredibly vulnerable.

Underneath the shields, our hearts harden and distance us from God's presence. God calls us into a loving, trusting relationship with Him. He wants us to trust Him to be our shield and our defender, our loving protector.

If we take matters into our own hands and pick up our own shields, we step outside of this trusting relationship — we get out of step with the Spirit. We leave the River. What are we to do? We must lay down our shield. We need to come to God with our anger and our hurt. We need to talk openly and honestly with Him about it, and we need to express to Him our willingness to lay down these shields and to trust Him. When you do that, your heart will begin to soften. Reaffirm your trust in His loving protection, and in the adequacy and sufficiency of His loving presence.

We need to obey Jesus' command to bless those who curse us. Pray blessings on the person who has hurt you. Pray all the good things you want in your life upon them. If you want to know God's love and God's peace, pray that for them. If you want to live in healthy relationships, ask God to help their relationships be healthy and fulfilling. As we pray blessings, our hearts soften further, and the shields come down more. We intentionally place ourselves in God's safe hands, and we can access His presence as we open our hearts.

I am not suggesting that you should allow yourself to be abused. I think you can have a soft heart and appropriate boundaries. Too often we opt for a hard heart to create inner boundaries that provide no true safety and actually harm our relationship with God. If we keep our hearts soft, we can become sensitive to the Spirit. We can begin to identify what it feels like for the water to drip off of our spirits as we start climbing out of the River.

Living in the River

There are certain times in life when we are more susceptible to getting out of step with the Spirit. We must know what those are, and we must take extra time during those particularly vulnerable seasons to get alone with God. These are like blinking yellow lights on a roadway — they are times to exercise caution or we will find ourselves out of the River. We may need to cancel some appointments on our calendar in order to create the space we need to get alone with Him. If we don't create the space in our calendar to meet with Him, we won't create the space in our souls for Him to work.

We may need to stay up most of the night in prayer to wrestle down our fears and surrender to God so we can find our way back into the River. We will certainly have to walk through those times slower. Our natural tendency is to speed up during times of chaos, but we must intentionally slow down. We must be at peace to lead in peace. We must be in the River to lead people into the presence of God.

I was preaching about this concept of living in the River of God at a conference in Pennsylvania. A man came up to me the day after I talked about becoming a full-time River Dweller. He was a Harley rider, and pretty much every stereotypical image that comes to mind when you think about a Harley rider was true of him. He was a large man, heavily tattooed, with a leather vest marked with Harley insignia.

The man put his large, meaty hands on my both my shoulders and spoke with a deep, husky voice. "Last night when you spoke about the River of God," he said, "I felt the Holy Spirit inside of me for the first time in my life." At this point, tears started flowing down his bearded cheeks.

He continued, "I woke up this morning, and I was still in the River. I went to work today, and I lived in the River of His presence all day at work. My work environment isn't exactly conducive to the things of God, but I was in the River all day."

Then he leaned even closer to me, and inches away from my face, he whispered through the tears: "Pray for me. I never want to get out of the River again."

I prayed, through tears of my own, that neither one of us would ever get out of the River. I prayed we would become so sensitive to the Spirit we could feel the water of the Spirit dripping off of us the moment we started climbing out onto the riverbanks. I prayed that leaving the River of God's presence would cut us so deeply to the heart that we would turn around right there on the spot and get back in. We would become full-time River Dwellers, living in the present fullness of the Spirit of God.

I want to live in the River of God's presence. I want to be in the River of God when I am in prayer and when I am eating dinner with my family. I want to be in the River of God's presence when I am in worship and when I am in a staff meeting at work. I want to be in the River of God when I am taking a slow, prayerful walk in nature and when I am in a high stakes leadership environment around a boardroom table in an atmosphere fraught with fear. I want to be in the River of Life when I am alone with God for days at the monastery and when I am in the middle of 50,000 people at a ball game. I don't ever want to get out of the River.

I want to become so sensitive to the Spirit's presence that I can sense the water dripping off of me as I begin to get out of the River of Life. I want the dripping water to be painful to my heart so that I quickly turn back to the River. I want to become so sensitive to what grieves Him that I immediately realize my misstep, repent, and jump back in. Too often, we get out of the River, and we aren't aware we have left the River behind. We wander to shore, and one day we wake up and realize we are deep in the woods. We look around and think to ourselves, "I know there was a River around here someplace."

I don't want to live in an inconsistent, interrupted flow of the Spirit's fullness in my life. I want to become so close to His heartbeat that I don't miss a whisper of the Spirit.   I want to be a full-time River Dweller, and I want to carry the Living Water to whomever I am with, so they too will hunger and thirst for the Living God. Isn't that what you want, too?

Reflection Questions

Chapter 4: Climbing out of the River

1. What does it feel like when you get out of the River? Can you recognize the signs and symptoms? Describe them. If you can't, begin to ask God for insight.

2. Are you currently walking in the light with God and others? Unconfessed sin gets us out of the River. Do you need to confess anything to God and others? To what degree do you receive light as a gift, versus an intrusion?

3. How do you consistently recognize and respond to the conviction of the Spirit?

4. Secrets disease the soul. Are you currently keeping secrets that are preventing you from experiencing the fullness of God? Will you bring those into the light with God and others?

5. Everyone has a dashboard of the soul. What are the indicator lights in your life that flash when you are getting out of the River? Take time to write down some of the gauges on your spiritual dashboard. Share those with others.

6. What are the shields you pull up to protect your heart — that not only block out pain, but block out God? Do you have any shields up currently that you need to lay down so you can give God access to your heart again? Describe them. Ask others to pray with you.

It is often at our worst moments when God does His best work.

"Above all else, guard your heart, for it is the wellspring of life."

Proverbs 4:23, NIV, 1984

CHAPTER 5

Twists in the River Bend

I am a passionate person, and I struggle with the Curse of the Passionate. The Curse of the Passionate is that it is never enough. No matter what you see, you always want to see more. No matter what you experience, you always want to experience more. As a passionate person, I can easily fall into the trap of never being satisfied.

Passionate people expect great things. The good news is because they expect great things, attempt great things, and have great resolve, passionate people tend to make things happen. The bad news is they are so expectant that they often don't pause to enjoy the results, as they should. They forget to take time to celebrate and to give thanks. They conquer one hill, and with a quick sigh of relief, they are running off to take the next. Success is never enough, and great expectation can lead to great disappointment.

Disappointment can cause any of us to harden our hearts and can lead us out of the River. Whether or not you are a passionate person, you will experience disappointments in your life. We must learn how to deal with disappointment if we are going to become full-time River Dwellers.

I am 49 years old as I write this, and I have noticed many people go through a midlife crisis somewhere between their midforties and midfifties. I think a midlife crisis is most often about disappointments that stack up and go unprocessed. When we are in our twenties and thirties, we have many dreams and ideals for our life. We have hopes of the way our life will turn out. We have a picture of what our ideal marriage will be like and what our kids will turn out to be like. We have pictures of a certain depth we will have in our relationships. We have ideals about our relationship with God — where it will take us, what we will experience, what we will see God do in and through us. We may have thoughts about our financial future or our retirement years. We have images of what our careers will produce, the difference we will make, and the legacy we will leave.

We work hard for these dreams. We trudge on vigorously through our thirties and into our forties, and we hold on to hope. There are bumps in the road and disappointments along the way, but we press on. Slowly we begin to realize all of our ideals are not going to come about exactly as we expected. Our marriage may be good, but it isn't all we hoped it would be. Our children are growing and maturing, but maybe not at the rate we would have liked, or maybe some of them have even chosen to wander from the ways of God, and our hearts are broken. Our career has good aspects, but maybe is not all that we had hoped for — we thought we would make more of a difference and that our life endeavors would be more fulfilling.

For many people the disappointments are fairly minor and are mixed with many blessings, and they process midlife with relative ease. For some, the disappointments are more significant. Maybe their expectations were higher or their processing wasn't as complete or they suffered more blows. For whatever reason, they get stuck in a pile of disappointments that threaten their River Dwelling existence.

When all of these disappointments begin to stack up on us, many people get out of the River completely. They wander deep into the woods of sin trying to recapture the energy and passion they once felt in their youth. They are on a quest to feel alive again, because so much has died within them. Often it isn't a conscious decision; it is an unidentified longing of the soul. I have grieved over many people's affairs and other immoral wanderings because of this illicit search for the fountain of youth.

Other people simply give up. They don't wander deep into the woods, but they do get out of the River. They sit alongside the riverbanks. They often become defeated, bitter, negative, critical people. Some become cynical people who find skepticism easier than optimism. They often unwittingly resist the next move of God, because they have gotten out of the River themselves. It is an equally unsatisfying place to be; there is no life there. Deep in the woods or alongside the riverbank is no way for a River Dweller to live.

These disappointments that stack up are like twists in the river bend. They are turns that you don't predict; paths that you don't plan for. The problem with these twists in the river bend is many people don't make the turn. Sometimes it is not a series of events, but one major catastrophe, like the death of a child or the death of a lifelong dream. My friend Martin Sanders refers to these events as "soul-robbing disappointments." Whether brought on by a catastrophic event or a series of events, this level of disappointment can threaten to rob us of our inheritance in the River of Life. We must learn to navigate these deep disappointments life brings us so that we can remain full-time River Dwellers.

My Soul-Robbing Disappointments

In the summer of 2013, I went through one of the darkest times of my life. I had a pile of disappointments stack up on me, both personally and professionally. As a church, we had taken a huge risk and bought a big piece of property in 2009. We were meeting in rented space, and we felt like it was time for a permanent home. At the time, we prayed and fasted about purchasing this land. I told our congregation that we needed to raise a "God only possible sum of money" to sustain the land and put a building there. I knew if God didn't do a miracle, we weren't going to get the job done.

As the leadership team prayed and fasted, we sensed God leading us to buy the land. We didn't jump into this risk recklessly. We had spiritually attuned, discerning people on the board, on the staff, on the leadership teams, and in the congregation who prayed, fasted, and waited on God over this decision. We were united that God was in it, and we took the risk. We purchased nearly 30 buildable acres in a step of faith.

Right as we purchased the land, the economy took a free fall, and many people left our church. We had less money, less people, and more debt than we could possibly manage. We trusted God, continued pursuing Him for a miracle, and put in our best human efforts — we gave generously, made significant sacrifices, and strategically planned our finances so we could take the next step and build on the land.

In the summer of 2013, almost four years after we purchased the land, we were closing in on a deal that would have enabled us to start phase one of our construction. The bottom began to fall out of the deal, and it didn't go through. It was a severe blow, and with it, a long-term dream was crashing to the ground.

On top of that, we had been pursuing revival for many years as a church. I remain convinced the moral fiber and spiritual foundation of our society has so deeply eroded that the only chance we have to turn around the church and the society is another Great Awakening. My calling has always been to lead, pray, fast, and preach toward revival. Jen and I pursued God and revival with great vigor, and we were not seeing the great move of God that we were seeking.

That same summer, as part of our pursuit of revival, Jen and I went on a missions trip to a place where God was pouring out His Spirit; we were both hoping and praying for a fresh touch from God. We saw many miracles, but the fresh touch we were personally hoping for did not come, and we were deeply disappointed again. As all that was occurring, Jen and I went through some personal crises in our lives that caused us great pain. More soul-robbing disappointments.

I have four promises from God that I have pursued passionately for many years. Promises that involve revival (which I wrote about in my book, *Pathways to the King*), our family, the property we stepped out in faith to purchase and God's provision for it and our church, and the books God called me to write. I have prayed over prophetic words about these promises for years. And none of them have come true yet. Disappointment after disappointment. They were stacking in my soul.

For the first time in my life, I wrestled with a question most of us do not want to articulate. I struggled with the question, "Does God lie?" The disappointments were damaging my trust with God. I knew I needed to process them, or I couldn't live in the River.

I called my buddy Ron and asked him to spend a day with me. We spent a whole day together, and I processed. I grieved. I expressed my disappointments, my anger, my hurt, my frustration, my longings, my heart, and my soul. We laughed, we cried, we yelled. He entered into my grief and carried the load with me. It was an incredible gift to me. I didn't need anyone to fix me. I didn't need anyone to tell me the right answers — I knew God didn't lie. It wasn't a theological crisis I was struggling with; it was a crisis of the soul.

I got home and processed some more with Jen. Jen's relationship with God has never come easy; she has struggled hard on her spiritual journey. That day, she said something that stuck. It wasn't just a moral platitude or religious slogan; it was a truth she knew after a hard-fought battle in her own soul. After listening to me empathetically, and through tears, she simply said, "He is the King; He can do what He wants."

I laughed and said, "Yeah, He can even lie if He wants!" But I knew she was right. I don't always understand God, but I know I can trust Him because of the cross. He isn't a God who sits in a comfortable, air conditioned Heaven while we sweat it out through Earth's hardships. He is a God who left that throne and entered into the hardship with us and for us. He was born in a stable and died on a cross in humiliation. He is a High Priest who understands our weakness, our temptations, our frailties, and our hardships. He is the God of the cross who can be trusted. I know He is good, no matter how bad life gets. It is always the cross I come back to, and it is always the cross that gives me hope no matter what may come my way.

The turning point that finally allowed me to navigate this river bend came in a time alone with God. Most life change occurs alone with God. The people in our life play an important role in our journey, and we need good friends to process with, grieve with, pray with, and cry with. But sooner or later, if we are going to get back in the River, we must get alone with God. As I look back on my journey, every one of my spiritual turning points was highlighted by a time alone with God where God spoke to me, or met me, or revealed something to me. This was no exception.

I felt drawn to the famous passage in Hebrews 11 — it is often referred to as the hall of faith. There are many stories about people who received promises from God. Some of them received results pretty quickly. Some of them waited for a long time, like Abraham and Sarah, who had a promise that God would give them a child in their old age. Eventually, after a painstakingly long waiting period of 25 years, the promise came. Those stories are all good, because the heroes received what was promised — and this gives us all hope, because we all want to see God deliver on His promises.

After telling us the stories of many heroes of the faith, the author starts to wrap up this legendary chapter with this paragraph:

> *"And what more shall I say? I do not have time to tell about Gideon, Barak, Samson and Jephthah, about David and Samuel and the prophets, who through faith conquered kingdoms, administered justice, and gained what was promised; who shut the mouths of lions, quenched the fury of the flames, and escaped the edge of the sword; whose weakness was turned to strength; and who became powerful in battle and routed foreign armies. Women received back their dead, raised to life again."* (Hebrews 11:32-35)

I love this story! These people all received promises, and God delivered every time. But the chapter doesn't end there. We continue in verse 35:

> *"There were others who were tortured, refusing to be released so that they might gain an even better resurrection. Some faced jeers and flogging, and even chains and imprisonment. They were put to death by stoning; they were sawed in two; they were killed by the sword. They went about in sheepskins and goatskins, destitute, persecuted and mistreated — the world was not worthy of them. They wandered in deserts and mountains, and in caves and holes in the ground."* (Hebrews 11:35-38)

Then this verse, which I had read casually too many times before, hit me like a punch: "These were all commended for their faith, yet none of them received what had been promised" (Hebrews 11:39).

I thought, "See, God does lie!" These folks held on to the promise of God, but they didn't receive what He promised. He even commended them for their faith, but they still didn't get the promise.

The next verse helped me see things in a new light: "God had planned something better for us so that only together with us would they be made perfect" (Hebrews 11:40). Now I saw it from Heaven's perspective.

God gave these people a promise, and they believed it. They held on to the promise. They prayed for the promise, and God commended them for their faith. They didn't realize the promise was not going to be fulfilled in their lifetime. Instead, they were fighting for a promise another generation would receive. They were commissioned by God to fight for a promise for the next generation. Now don't miss this: God could have told them the promise wasn't for them; He knew they thought it was for them, but He didn't bother clarifying that. He said nothing; He let them believe it, He let them fight for it, and He commended them for their belief. But they never received their promise. They fought the fight for a future generation, even though they didn't realize it. God knew they were disappointed, but He still didn't clarify they were fighting for a future promise; He simply cheered them on and commended them. Of course, they got their reward in Heaven, and the next generation got to stand on the ground that they had battled for.

As I read this, I knew the question God was asking me deep in my spirit: "Will you fight for your promises even if you don't get to see them in your lifetime? Will you fight for the future generations?" And that day, once again, I surrendered to the King, and I vowed I would. I will battle for revival until my final breath, even if I don't get to taste of its riches. I will battle for the sake of the King and His future generations. I will battle for the promises He has given me, because I believe them to my core, and I know that either in my generation or in a future generation, His promises will be fulfilled. But, for now, not knowing the outcome, I simply had to surrender and say "yes" to the assignment that God had given me.

Peace always follows surrender. Where there is no surrender, there is no peace. Where there is no surrender, there is no way to dwell in the River. An unsurrendered heart stops up the flow of the River of Life.

I have received many promises from God. I do not know which of these I will see fulfilled in my lifetime. I suspect some of them will not be fulfilled until a future generation, and others will only partially be fulfilled in my lifetime. I am not living for myself. I am living for the King and His Kingdom. I am willing to fight the battle today that could allow the next generation to live in the promises I have claimed. If you read this, and you are younger than me, I am fighting for you. I want your generation to experience the great awakening that I am battling for. If those in their midlife crisis do not learn to process their disappointments and fight for the next generation, then they will be become bitter and cynical and fail to pass on the promise that God entrusted to them.

Battling Disappointments

There are a few core principles that can help you survive the soul-robbing disappointments that threaten your life as a River Dweller. First, remember God redeems suffering. In this broken and fallen world, there will be suffering. Sadly, there is no way to escape it this side of Heaven. Apart from the cross, suffering can be endured at best. In the light of the cross, suffering cannot only be endured; it can be redeemed. Only the work of Christ on the cross can take the worst that this world has to offer and turn it into the best place for God to display His redeeming grace and power.

In Romans 8:28-29 Paul writes, "And we know that in all things God works for the good of those who love him, who have been called according to his purpose. For those God foreknew he also predestined to be conformed to the image of his Son, that he might be the firstborn among many brothers and sisters."

This passage teaches us that God can take everything in our life and use it to make us like Jesus — this is God's predetermined purpose for your life and mine, that we grow up to be like Jesus. This doesn't mean He approves of everything that comes into our life or that He sent every bad thing. God can take abuse and redeem it to make us more like Jesus. He would never desire that anyone be abused. It is evil, and God doesn't desire evil. God is so good, and Jesus' death on the cross is so powerfully redemptive, that God can take even the worst things that life throws at us and make something good out of them.

This concept leaves us with perpetual hope. No matter where our circumstances take us, we are never beyond the redemptive reach of God. I think we spend too much time asking the wrong question in the face of suffering. We ask, "Why?" Why did this happen to me? Why did God allow this? Why didn't God stop this? But God never promises to answer that question. Often, questioning the "why" leads us into accusation against God. It can actually harden our hearts. Instead, I try to focus my quest of

Why into .

understanding around the question, "How?" How can God redeem this in my life? How can God make me more like Jesus through this? This is a question God has promised to answer in James 1:2-5:

> *"Consider it pure joy, my brothers and sisters, whenever you face trials of many kinds, because you know that the testing of your faith produces perseverance. Let perseverance finish its work so that you may be mature and complete, not lacking anything. If any of you lacks wisdom, you should ask God, who gives generously to all without finding fault, and it will be given to you."*

James urges us in times of trials to rejoice, because God can redeem our circumstances to mature us. James is in agreement with Paul's thinking in Romans 8, but James adds this idea: if you don't know how God can redeem a hardship to mature you, then ask Him. He will give you wisdom. God will show you how He can take a tragic event and turn it into a triumph for your faith and maturity.

Whenever you go through a difficult trial, claim these two passages, and ask God to show you how He will redeem the difficult circumstances in your life to make you more like Jesus. God will always deliver when you are on this quest. The redeeming nature of God gives us hope and direction for the dark times in life. God has guided me to maturity through a marriage crisis and troubles with my kids. God has guided me through church crisis and personal crisis. God redeemed the crisis I went through when I wrestled with the question, "Does God lie?" And God will redeem the next dark season of my life. He will redeem your dark seasons, too, if you take Him at His word. Focusing on God's redemptive work will keep you in the River.

The Dark Night of the Soul

When you're in the midst of soul-robbing disappointments, here's another principle that will help you stay in the River: keep doing the right things. If you do the right things, eventually you will get the right results. I think that is a proverbial statement. It is generally the way life works. So even when you are in the dark seasons of life, keep doing the right things. Often in the dark we are tempted to give up. We are hurt, and we often respond by giving up; we get out of the River and sit on the riverbank.

In the midst of my dark season when I was wresting with whether God lies, I went through a dark night of the soul that lasted for many months. People sometimes use that expression to describe a hard time. But Saint

John of the Cross, who wrote about the dark night of the soul, wasn't referring to hardship. He described it as the absence of God. This isn't an absence brought on by sin or our human choices. We have not quenched or grieved the Spirit. We have not wandered out of the River. The dark night of the soul is an absence of God's presence that God chooses. He darkens our senses so we can no longer monitor the Spirit's presence and activity in our life. We become like a pilot flying through the clouds without the use of the instruments.

In the midst of this deep struggle that I found myself in, God seemed to disappear. Even after I read that Hebrews passage and surrendered, the presence of God did not return. I have lived most of my adult life with a keen sense of the presence of God. It has always been easy for me, since that first filling of the Spirit, to enter into God's presence. I could be in a stadium full of 50,000 screaming fans, and pause for a moment, and sense God's presence. I have cultivated this awareness of the Spirit. I have coveted His presence and pursued Him vigorously most of my adult life. But, for the first time in my life, for an extended period of time, God was nowhere to be found. I would pray, but He was distant. I would meditate on Scripture, but He seemed absent, and the breath of God was hard to come by. I would worship, but there was no sense of the presence of God. I prayed the Psalms, which had helped me through so many dark times in my past, but still I had no sense that God was near.

Fortunately, I had read St. John of the Cross's work, *Dark Night of the Soul*, and I had read R. Thomas Ashbrook's book, *Mansions of the Heart*. The first time I read Ashbrook's book, I was at the monastery. I had been experiencing a great season of life in the River at that time. God's presence was more tangible and His voice more steady and clear at that time than any other. I was deep in the River and enjoying it thoroughly. As I read through the book and it talked about deeper union with God, I resonated with so much of what Ashbrook wrote. He described some things that I had never heard anyone else talk about, but that I was experiencing personally.

For example, Ashbrook explained when we get into the upper mansions of intimacy with God, sometimes we are drawn to pray without words. Even when we pray for others, we will feel compelled to pray without words. I had been experiencing this for some time and one day found myself in a class environment at the seminary where we were praying for people. During the ministry time, I felt the Spirit drawing me to pray for Dianna Sanders, Martin's wife. It is not uncommon for us to float around the room and lay hands on people during certain ministry times in our classes. We follow the leading of the Spirit and lay hands on those to whom the Spirit calls us. So, this day, I felt the Spirit prompting me to go lay hands on Dianna.

I just entered into Jesus' presence as I laid hands on her, but I didn't pray anything. I sat with her in God's presence in silence.

A few days later, Martin called and asked me about it. He wanted to know what I prayed for Dianna. I said, "Nothing." He said, "What do you mean, nothing?" I said, "I didn't pray anything." He said, "You can't pray nothing." I said, "I simply laid my hand on her and entered into Jesus' presence. Then I sat with her in Jesus' presence. Why do you ask?" He told me that Dianna experienced the presence and power of God surging through her like electricity. I said, "That was Jesus." I have nothing. I have no power. I have no magic. I cannot produce spiritual results on my own. My words in prayer cannot create new realities. All I can do when I pray for someone is to look to Jesus. It was simply Jesus' presence.

Ashbrook talked about praying like this — simply entering into the presence of God and carrying people to the presence of God without words. I'd never heard anyone talk about it; I had simply stumbled upon it by living in the River. It was a movement of the Spirit in my life. After I read that chapter, I couldn't wait to see what lay beyond the veil. What great mystery did God have for me next? I wanted to know what was coming down the road in my journey, so I eagerly looked ahead to the next chapter to see what God had for me.

The next chapter was on the dark night of the soul. It described a season where I would not sense God's presence, and He would seem absent. I read it and was so deeply troubled by what may lie ahead for me that I went out for a quiet walk with God in the woods. I sobbed. I wept as I walked and said to the Lord, "I have been in your presence so long, I can't imagine living without you. I have cultivated Your presence my whole life. I don't want to be without Your presence. Please." I heard the Spirit gently whisper to me, "Even if you cannot feel me, am I not still with you? You can trust me."

It was several years later I found myself in that dark night of the soul. Even though I did not sense God's presence, I kept doing the right things. I kept praying. I kept worshiping. I kept reading and meditating on Scripture. I kept spending time alone with God. I probably spent more time in silence than ever before. I just sat waiting for Him. As He had hidden Himself, I knew that one day He would reveal Himself once again. I fundamentally believe that if you do the right things, eventually you'll get the right results. It is the law of the harvest. A person reaps what they sow — for good or for bad.

As you seek to be a full-time River Dweller, you may find yourself in a dark night of the soul. You must continue doing the right things even if you don't sense any results. It's a key part of staying in the River.

When trouble comes our way, we can only respond in one of three ways.

We can rebel, we can resign, or we can surrender. When we rebel, we shake our fist at God and go our own way. We get angry, and we choose to defy God. Rebellion is a road that leads to darkness, and darkness is destructive. There is no life-giving water along this path.

When we resign, we give up. We sit on the riverbanks and say to God, "You are bigger; You are more powerful. There is nothing I can do. I quit." This attitude doesn't lead us to peace. It more likely leads us to depression. Again, there is no life-giving water here.

Resignation and rebellion are both rooted in distrust. This is why we must process our disappointments, or we will end up with distrust in our soul which leads to a rebellion or resignation — we will either end up in the woods or on the riverbanks.

Surrender, though, is rooted in trust. We say, "Lord, I don't understand. I know I can trust you because of the cross. I know you are a God who understands pain and darkness, and I know you love me. So, I surrender." Surrender keeps our heart soft before the Lord. Rebellion and resignation harden our hearts. The Proverb writer exhorted us: "Above all else, guard your heart, for it is the wellspring of life" (Proverbs 4:23, NIV, 1984).

Guard your heart, above all else. It is priority number one. Before you do anything else, guard your heart. We must keep our heart soft, humble, and contrite before the Lord — especially during times of hardship. When life gets hard, our hearts often harden with it — unless we fight the battle for the heart. The soft heart is a surrendered heart.

Saint John of the Cross says the dark night is a time of purgation. God redeems our suffering to purify us. A new level of purification always precedes our next level of intimacy with God. We must embrace it.

Hebrews 12:14 says, "Without holiness no one will see the Lord." There is certainly an eschatological meaning to this text. Unless Jesus purifies us, we won't get to Heaven and see God. Only through faith in Christ can our souls be purified, so that we can enter Heaven. There is also a present reality to this text. Before our next level of intimacy with God, we must be willing to embrace a new level of holiness. God is loving, but drawing near requires purification. The dark night of the soul is about purgation — God redeems the darkness to lead us into a new level of holiness, if we are willing. We must embrace this work of the Spirit if we are going to dwell in the River even in the darkness. Though we cannot feel Him or sense Him, we can still dwell in the River.

I discovered through the dark night of the soul that my faith became deeper. This was ironic, because I had struggled with faith more deeply in this time than at any other time in my life. The dark night is about believing when we do not see, when we do not feel, and when we do not understand.

We hold on to what God tells us even while we have no evidence of it. Never forget what God has told you in the light when you are wandering in the darkness. The dark night of the soul is a time to hold on to the things God has told us in the light. Even if the evidence of His presence is temporarily removed, and if we process it well, with a soft, surrendered heart, God redeems the dark night to deepen our faith. If we rebel or resign, we miss out on the very thing that God brought to mature us and take us to our next level of intimacy. Too often we pray for the next level of intimacy, but we reject the answer to prayer that could take us there. We must see the darkness as a pathway to new depth with God, not as a punishment for wrongdoing.

Not only did I discover that the dark night deepened my faith, but I also discovered God in the midst of it. It was different than I had ever experienced before, but He was there — just as He told me He would be. I could no longer sense Him or feel Him. And I couldn't hear Him — He went silent on me. I could feel the effects of His presence still, if I looked for it carefully. It was like the sun behind the clouds. You can't see the sun when it is behind the clouds. You can't feel the same level of warmth that it produces on a bright and clear day. You can feel some warmth; you can still feel the effects of the sun radiating through the clouds. There is still light — it isn't like when the sun goes down for the night, because it manages to make its way through the clouds and lighten our world. It isn't as bright as a cloudless day, but it is still light brought about by the sun's presence.

The presence of God in the dark night is like pulling up blankets on a cold night. Sometimes when it is cold out, Jen and I will stack blankets on our bed (because we are too cheap to turn up the heat!). We have a thick pile of blankets, topped off with a quilt, and when we get into bed feeling chilly, we grab the blankets and pull them up to our chin. At first you can feel the weight of the blankets as you lay there. But eventually you don't feel the weight any longer; you just feel the warmth — you feel the effect of the blankets. This is what I discovered about the presence of God in the dark night of the soul: I could no longer sense His presence, but I could feel the effects of His presence. As I continued to do the right things, and as I battled for a soft heart, I could feel His peace. It was the old, familiar, supernatural peace of the River. It wasn't accompanied with other familiar signs of His presence that I had come to know, but the peace was there. I also knew deep within my soul that He loved me. I didn't feel His love like I had in times past. I didn't hear Him speak to me about it, but I knew it deep within me. I was learning to walk in the dark. If I had stopped doing the right things, and rebelled out in the woods or resigned on the riverbanks,

I suspect I would have lost the effects of His presence.

David wrote in Psalm 63:8, "I cling to you; your right hand upholds me." He was going through a dark season. He was literally and spiritually in a desert. His heart longed for God: "Earnestly I seek you; I thirst for you, my whole being longs for you, in a dry and parched land where there is no water" (verse 1). He longed for previous experiences that He had with God. He kept doing the right things in the darkness — he cried out to God; he sought Him in the night. David clung to God with a soul desperation, and God's right hand upheld him.

When we are under the crushing weight of sadness and disappointment and the dark night of the soul, we must look for the right hand of God upholding us, because it will be hidden from us in the dark. It will not be obvious to us, like at other times. But if we look, we will find it there. We will find it on some occasions in the touch of a friend. At other times we will find the right hand of God upholding us through a song that cuts through all the darkness and ministers directly to our spirits. Sometimes we will spot the hand of God in the dark through a hardy laugh in the midst of harsh grief. If we look, we will find the strong right hand of God upholding us even in the darkness — it will be a glimpse of hope breaking through like a ray of light ever so slightly illuminating the darkness.

The Battle of Perspective

One final thought about battling through dark times: we must fight for the right perspective. Perspective is a little thing that makes a big difference. Perspective does not change our circumstances, but it does change us. If we hold on to the wrong perspective for too long, it will ruin our souls. We must battle for the right perspective.

It is easy to become overwhelmed by the darkness of these times. It is easy to fix on what we lack, what we are missing, what is going wrong, and what we wish we had. We can become ungrateful people, grumbling like the children of Israel in their desert experience. In the end, it wasn't their desert experience that robbed them; it was their perspective that robbed them of all God had for them. This is what I discovered I had to do to win the battle for perspective: Grieve the bad; thank God for the good; and hold on to the eternal perspective. This will enable you to see in the dark.

I think we spend too much time trying to control our outer world rather than trying to win the battle for our inner world. We try to control people and circumstances and outcomes. When we get fixated on controlling our outer world, we feel anxious, upset, irritated, aggravated, and annoyed. It gets us out of the River. If we win the battle for perspective, the battle of the inner world, then even if our outer world is chaotic, our inner world can be at peace and we can discover contentment that comes from resting in God.

To win the battle of perspective, we have to grieve the bad. There are a lot of things in life that don't work out the way we want. This is a dark and disappointing world. It is grievous to God Himself — sin grieves the Holy Spirit. This world isn't working the way He wants it to work. He grieves when people are abused, raped, murdered, and abandoned. He grieves when children are trafficked, aborted, and neglected. He grieves over wars, injustice, poverty, gender bias, and racism. He grieves over broken marriages, domestic violence, and financial ruin. This side of Heaven, everything is not working out the way God intended it to. That doesn't mean God is a frustrated old man in Heaven who doesn't know what to do. He still moves history to His ultimate ends. But, God never designed sin, and He doesn't condone it. It is evil, and He grieves its presence in this life. When sin and its effects touch our lives, we need to grieve. We also need to hold on to hope, because He can redeem all of these evils. There is always hope in the light of the cross.

Grieving the pains and losses of life is a form of homesickness. It reminds us we are strangers passing through this land, but our ultimate home is in Heaven where our true citizenship resides. We are longing for Heaven, where evil will be dealt its final deathblow. This is why Jesus taught us to pray, "Your kingdom come; your will be done, on earth as it is in heaven." I have heard people argue, in the name of God's sovereignty, that rape or molestation was God's will. Sin is never God's will. Thankfully, God can redeem it so we have hope, but He didn't will it. So we have to grieve even while we hang on to hope.

Some people never give themselves time, space, and permission to grieve. This is not conducive to navigating our way around this tricky bend in the river; it will lead us to soul problems that obstruct our River Dwelling. Other people never get out of the grieving stage, because they never take time to focus on the good. They get stuck grieving over what they lost, or what they never had, and their eyes get fixed on themselves. If we are going to make it around this turn in the river bend, we must get our eyes on God and the good gifts He gives. And there is always good.

We need to give thanks. In hard times, praising God and giving thanks is a discipline. We have to be intentional about it, because for most of us, it will not flow naturally. If we get stuck on the bad, and never give thanks for the good, we will lose hope and never find our way to the River. All of our grumbling and lack of gratitude will contribute to our distrust, and eventually lead to resignation or rebellion and a hardened heart. We must give thanks. The darker the hour, the more thanksgiving is required. There are two times to give thanks: When we feel like it, and when we don't. We need to give thanks most precisely when we don't feel like it.

David practices grieving and thanksgiving in the Psalms. He wrestles with the darkness of life. He grieves it. He is raw with his emotions, and I love that about him. But he always ends with a surrendered heart of faith, trust, praise, and thanksgiving.

When I went through my dark season in 2013, I spent time every day grieving. I have a prayer journal on my computer, and I worked through my hurts, my disappointments, my emotions, and my grief with God. I was angry. I was sad. I was disappointed. I was discouraged. I felt it, I named it, and I grieved it. But then after each prayer session where I processed my grief, I ended with a time of thanksgiving. I recalled all the good things in my life. Every day I tried to find the good things in life — I looked for the hidden hand of God upholding me, and I thanked God for those things, and I intentionally tried to enjoy them.

Jen and I upped the "fun factor" in our life during that dark season. It was very intentional. David wrote, "Taste and see that the Lord is good" (Psalm 34:8). He wrote this during a very dark season in his own life. He had fled from Saul, and escaped to the land of the Philistines. The people knew who David was, because he had slain Goliath, so they handed him over to the king. He had to feign insanity to escape. He gives God thanks and praise in the Psalm for his deliverance, but it isn't like he landed on easy street. He was still without a home, and was on every wanted poster in Israel. Yet David took time to rejoice, give thanks, and celebrate the good things in life. We often lose sight of God's goodness in life's difficulties.

So in the summer of 2013, Jen and I deliberately engaged in more fun activities and intentionally gave thanks for these things because every good gift comes from above. We took more slow walks in beautiful places, and we intentionally noted the beauty and were deliberately thankful. We spent more time enjoying the good foods life offers, and carefully savored them while intentionally giving thanks. We took more trips, visited new places, experienced new things, and enjoyed each and every one of them as a good gift from God, and we gave Him thanks. With every new experience, and every thankful prayer, our hearts were lightened and we were made aware of the goodness of God. Light came to our dark places. It was because of the darkness, not in spite of it, that I became more appreciative of the people around me that I love, more grateful for the good things in life that I enjoy.

Grieve the bad, give thanks for the good, and battle for the eternal perspective. *Heaven will resolve all of Earth's problems and fulfill all of God's promises.* I love that. The older I get, the more I look forward to Heaven because of that truth. So often in the dark seasons of life, we act as if this life is all there is. It's not. Peter says we are "foreigners and exiles" in the world' (1 Peter 2:11). Paul says that "our citizenship is in heaven" (Philippians 3:20). We are just passing through. This is a temporary residence.

Imagine living in a temporary residence while you had your permanent dwelling place, your dream house, built. You wouldn't expect that your temporary residence would fulfill all the expectations of your dream house. You would endure the difficulties and disappointments of the temporary residence with a bit of patience and even joy, because you would look forward to the dream house. In the midst of experiencing the inconveniences of the temporary, you would remind yourself of the benefits of the dream house so that you would endure with joy. Whatever dream house you build on earth is still subject to the decay of this fallen world, but your home in Heaven is permanent and perfect. This is where your true citizenship lies. How easy it is for us to lose sight of this — especially when hardship comes our way. We will never control all of the outcomes on earth, but Heaven will resolve all of earth's problems and fulfill all of God's promises.

To gain perspective, I encourage you to take a slow walk through a cemetery once in a while. In the last month, I took two walks through a nearby cemetery. I did this intentionally to detach from the things of this world, and to attach more deeply to the eternal realm of my permanent citizenship. Cemeteries are often beautifully manicured places, and they make for peaceful walks on a pleasant afternoon. I walked through slowly, meditatively, and gratefully. As I walked through, I gave thanks to God for all the good things of life. I wanted to taste and see His goodness to me. Jen often walks with me, and we hold hands as we soak in the beauty of creation, and enjoy God's good gifts to us.

I also walked through reflectively. The first thing I gleaned from my reflective walk was that everyone dies. It seems obvious, but we lose sight of this too often. We live like this is all there is, and we fight for the outcomes in the here and now, all the while losing the eternal perspective. I wonder how many things we get hung up about on Earth that won't matter a bit 100 years after we are dead. Walking through a cemetery slowly and reflecting helps me right size life's problems. I kept my eyes on God as I walked and gave thanks for His eternal outlook on the world. As I did, I let go of my troubles, and His rest filled my soul.

I also noticed there aren't many famous people in cemeteries. I walked through one cemetery near my home, and I noticed one man was a congressmen for nearly 30 years over a century ago. I am a history buff, but I had never heard of the guy. I passed his tombstone twice in the past month, and I still can't remember his name. I'm sure during his lifetime he was important, had influence, and affluence, but 100 years after he died, no one remembers him. That helps me. It reminds me I have to link my life to the eternal purposes of God. Only that which lasts forever ultimately matters. It helps me to let go of those mounting pressures to make things happen that so often build up in my soul. As I walked, I let go of pressure and the need to make things happen. I took myself less seriously and took God more seriously. It gave me perspective.

Finally, in the cemetery I noticed everyone was buried with his or her family. Jesus said love God and love people — this is what matters most. When you get to the end of life, it is all that will matter. It is so simple. Why do we make it so complicated? As I walked slowly through the graveyard, I found myself feeling grateful for Jen. I thought about her and my kids and how much I loved them. My heart was gladdened. I started taking inventory of the people in my life for whom I am grateful. There are so many. Take a walk slowly through a graveyard. Reflect on what matters most in life, and orient yourself toward God and His eternal purposes. It truly gives you perspective.

✓Disappointments are inevitable. As you're seeking to be a full-time River Dweller, you will experience soul-robbing disappointments, and you may experience a dark night of the soul. While I was writing this book, my dear friend Martin Sanders lost his wife after a long bout with a terminal illness. We had prayed and fasted for her healing for a long time. It was yet another twist in the river bend. They come. Jesus told us in this world we would have trouble. But He also promised us that the Spirit would be in us like a River, a River of Life. To stay in the River, you must hold firm to the promise that God redeems suffering, you must keep doing the right things, and you must fight for the battle of perspective. Our perspective doesn't change our circumstances, but it does change us. It lightens our burdens and strengthens our grip on what matters most. Battle for the right perspective, and stay dwelling in the River. There are so few things that really matter for all eternity. Focus on those, and don't let the rest of the details of life drag you away from the River.

After many months of living in the dark night of the soul, I was with Jen one morning and just broke down and wept. Through my tears I said to her, "I just miss Him so much." The dark night made me appreciate the good things of this life more than I ever had. It strengthened my faith. It made me homesick. I longed for Him, and I longed for my eternal home. My heart hurt with longing. Shortly after that day, the sun broke through the clouds, and the presence of God returned. It has been intermittent, and He is still mostly silent at this point, but I can sense Him with me regularly once again. At times the presence of God is so tangible, it moves me to tears. I love His presence.

You can stay in the River even when the presence of God seems to disappear. It is almost like the River runs shallow in places. If we stay in the riverbed, and we keep doing the right things, sooner or later we will be back in the place where the River flows free and full once again.

Reflection Questions

Chapter 5: Twists in the River Bend

1.   What are the disappointments that have stacked up in your life? Have you processed and grieved those well?

2.   How do you process suffering? Do you take offense at God and withdraw and put up shields? Do you fixate on the "why" question? Or do you actively trust God to redeem your suffering? Recall a time in your life where you suffered and benefited from it, a time where you grew through the suffering. If you're in a group, share your experiences.

3.   Have you ever experienced a dark night of the soul? What was it like? Were you able to find God in the midst of it? Will you resolve to keep doing the right things even in the darkness?

4.   How do you fight for the right perspective during times of difficulty? What helps you to win the battle for perspective?

5.   If you are currently in a season of darkness, are there any adjustments that you can make now to help you live victoriously and in the River?

Grief or Mourn

Conclusion

Years ago Jen and I went tubing down a river in upstate New York. Sitting in our black tire tubes, we locked arms and let the river take us downstream.

There were places where the river flowed wildly, and we were tossed and turned in our tire tubes. The ride was adventurous, even a tad dangerous at times. At one point Jen was holding onto my tube, and we went over a waterfall. She was first, and as she dropped out of sight with a shriek, she pulled my tube right out from under me. Before I knew it, I was plunging over the waterfall without a tube.

The water was flowing so fast I couldn't stop. Every time I tried to stand, the rapids knocked me over. Finally, I decided to just let the current drag me along. I went with the flow. I came away with a few bruises, cuts, and scrapes from hitting rocks along the way. I have to admit, in hindsight, I loved the excitement of it all. But it was painful, too.

The river finally slowed down, and I was able to get back in my tube. Jen and I linked arms again, and I held on a little tighter this time. We drifted along through some places where the water flowed lazily, and we just relaxed in our tubes. We enjoyed the scenery and each other's company, the warmth of the sun, and the cool of the river. The water felt refreshing, even healing to my cuts and scrapes. The rest was pleasant after the white-water excitement we had been through.

There were a few places where the river ran shallow, and we had to get out of the tube and walk along the riverbed, until the water picked up once again, and the adventure continued. There were even a few places where we went around a river bend and had to duck out of the way of low-hanging branches and couldn't see what was coming next.

Sometimes my spiritual journey feels like this tire tube trip. I have been through the rapids when the Holy Spirit was doing supernaturally powerful things, and I was just along for the ride trying to hold on. At times, the Spirit was a bit surprising, a little unpredictable, perhaps even a little wild and scary. I have learned to enjoy the ride and the thrill of His power. I love seeing the power of rapid moving water, especially the rapids of the River of Life. Sometimes God manifests His presence; when He does, He leaves His mark. I long for more of those times for the sake of the Kingdom's advance.

There are times when the River seemed to slow down and flow along easily, gently, and the Spirit of God brought rest to my soul. I got to enjoy the goodness of God. I discovered His restorative presence in all of its healing qualities and sweetness. I have discovered I can't live at a constant turbulent pace. I need these quiet seasons, these refreshing, restorative waters of His presence. I need both the rapids and lazy waters in order to live a full, rich, River Dwelling life.

I have been in some shallow waters where the water flowed at a trickle. I had to pick up my tube and walk for a while. Whenever I followed the Riverbed, the water would eventually flow strong once again.

I've had to navigate a few tricky bends in the River, too. Some of them were dark and eerie places with dangerous, low-hanging branches and low visibility. If I just stayed in the River, eventually I came around the bend. I've learned even these parts of the journey serve their purpose in shaping me. It is often in these dry and shallow waters my longing for His presence and for the deeper waters increases.

Navigating these waters is all part of the River Dwelling experience. Jesus promised the Spirit would flow like a River within you. It is the River of Life. It offers you Living Water. Here you can find the soul-satisfying presence of God. You were born to be a full-time River Dweller. You were redeemed to live in and drink from this Living Water. Jesus invites you to come to the River. Dwell in the River. Stay in the River. Everything that touches the River lives.

Remember: God doesn't fill you with His Spirit just for your own benefit — He wants you to be a conduit of His Living Water. It is His desire that you carry this Living Water to a world dying of thirst, just like the early disciples did. Imagine a day when the vast majority of Christians spend the vast majority of their time dwelling in the River of Life. What difference would that make in the world?

Imagine the church was alive with Living Water and walking in the fullness of the Spirit. The people of God witnessed freely and powerfully out of the overflow of the goodness of God in their lives. They walked in supernatural power and carried the presence of God so formidably that everywhere they went, darkness was dissipated in their presence. Answers to prayer were plentiful. Miracles flowed. The message of Good News they freely received and freely offered transformed people on a daily basis. Churches brimmed with freshly redeemed lives. The people of God lived a supernatural adventure following the leadings of the Spirit into whatever divine appointments He had readied for them.

Imagine what a force the church could be if it were filled with full-time River Dwellers. It would flood the world with Living Water, and dying people would live, lost people would be found, thirsty people would be satisfied, broken people would be mended, sick people would be healed, and Jesus would be glorified. This is life in the River. We need the River of Life. Only in the River can the church close in on zero — the one number most precious to the One who died so we could live.

May you know the life of God flowing within you! May you be a full-time River Dweller in the River of Life where the fullness of God flows!

AMEN

Wind Fire Rain
River & Life

About the Author

 Rev. Dr. Rob Reimer is the Founding and Lead Pastor of South Shore Community Church, a church of the Christian and Missionary Alliance in Brockton, Massachusetts. Under Rob's leadership, what began as a small group of eight believers mobilized on mission to start a new church, resulting in hundreds of people coming to faith in Christ. Many of the examples and stories in this book come from the lessons learned from planting and leading a church in New England — one of the most unchurched regions in the nation.

In addition to his role as Lead Pastor, Rob is also a Field Pastor for the Christian and Missionary Alliance Field in Senegal, where he speaks and ministers to missionaries on a regular basis, encouraging and equipping them for service in a Muslim territory.

In his role as Global Leadership Associate, Rob travels internationally to train and equip Christian leaders for the work of ministry, focusing on assisting pastors in addressing issues within their souls so that they will be fully functional, healthy leaders who are able to influence others.

A gifted preacher and communicator, Rob preaches weekly at South Shore Community Church and is a sought-after speaker. He regularly speaks at conferences, leadership retreats, mission fields, churches, and seminaries in the United States and abroad. His sermons are posted online and are accessed by people around the world.

Rob is also an experienced teacher. He is an Adjunct Professor at Alliance Theological Seminary (ATS) in Nyack, NY, where he teaches Soul Care at the doctoral level and has taught various classes at the masters level, including Personal, Professional and Theological Foundations for Ministry; Evangelism; Mentoring; Pastoral Methods; Person in Ministry; Soul Care; and Intimacy and Authority.

Rob was ordained as a Minister of the Gospel of Jesus Christ by the Christian and Missionary Alliance in 1993. He earned a bachelor's degree in English from King's College, a Master's of Divinity from Alliance Theological Seminary, and a Doctorate in Preaching from Gordon-Conwell Theological Seminary.

Rob and his wife, Jen, live in the Bridgewater, MA area with their four children, Danielle, Courtney, Darcy, and Craig.

You can access Rob's sermons and speaking itinerary on his website, www.DrRobReimer.com

If you like this book, you may also be interested in
PATHWAYS TO THE KING
Living a Life of Spiritual Renewal and Power

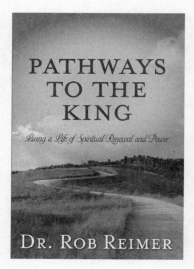

We need revival. The church in America desperately needs revival. There are pockets of it happening right now, but we need another Great Awakening. About forty years ago, the church was impacted by the church growth movement. The goal of the movement was to get the church focused on the Great Commission — taking the Good News about Jesus to the entire world. The church was off mission, and the movement was a necessary course correction. But it didn't work. Many people came to Christ as a result of this outreach emphasis, and I am grateful for that. More churches are now focused on evangelism, helping people come to know Jesus, than they were before the movement. But we have fewer people attending church now (percentage wise) than ever before in the history of the United States. We need revival.

This book is about how we can usher in revival and also about the price that we must pay to experience it. I believe we have a part to play in seeing the next great spiritual awakening. God wants us to be carriers of His Kingdom. He wants us to experience the reality and fullness of His Kingdom, and he wants us to expand the Kingdom to others — just like Jesus did. In order to do that, I believe we must follow 8 Kingdom Pathways of Spiritual Renewal: Personalizing our Identity in Christ, Pursuing God, Purifying Ourselves, Praising, Praying Kingdom Prayers, Claiming Promises, Passing the Tests, and Persisting. These 8 pathways are discussed in great detail, are securely rooted in biblical truths, and are illustrated by compelling examples from Scripture and from my life, the lives of believers in my community, and in the lives of great Christians throughout history.

Available at **www.DrRobReimer.com**